Writing Class

Writing Class

The Kootenay School of Writing Anthology

ANDREW KLOBUCAR

AND MICHAEL BARNHOLDEN,

EDITORS

New Star Books

VANCOUVER

1999

Introduction © 1999 Andrew Klobucar and Michael Barnholden.

New Star Books Ltd.
107 · 3477 Commercial Street
Vancouver, BC V5N 4E8
www.NewStarBooks.com

Designed and typeset at The Cardigan Press
Printed & bound in Canada by Hignell Printing

1 2 3 4 5 03 02 01 00 99

Publication of this work is made possible by grants from the Canada Council, the British Columbia Arts Council, and the Department of Canadian Heritage Book Publishing Industry Development Program.

CANADIAN CATALOGUING
IN PUBLICATION DATA

Main entry under title:
Writing class
Poems.
Includes bibliographical references.

ISBN 0-921586-68-x

1. Canadian poetry (English) – British Columbia.*
2. Canadian poetry (English) – 20th century.*
I. Klobucar, Andrew, 1967–
II. Barnholden, Michael, 1951–
III. Kootenay School of Writing.

PS8295.5.B7W74 1999   C811'.5408'09711
C99-911059-4
PR9198.2.B72W74 1999

The editors are grateful to the following poets and their publishers for permission to reprint copyrighted work: Lary Bremner (Timewell), from "Ruck"; Gerald Creede, "Résumé" from *Ambit*, Tsunami Editions; Peter Culley, "Winterreisse," "A Letter From Hammertown to East Vancouver and the East Village," and "Fruit Dots" from *The Climax Forest*, Leech Books; Kevin Davies, from *Pause Button*, Tsunami Editions; Dennis Denisoff, "A Comprehensive Miner Murders the Code" from *Tender Agencies*, Arsenal Pulp Press; Jeff Derksen, "Interface" from *Dwell*, Talonbooks; Dan Farrell, "Thinking of You" from *Thimking of You*, Tsunami Editions; Kathryn MacLeod, "The Infatuation," "Asylum," and "One Hour Out of Twenty-four" from *Mouthpiece*, Tsunami Editions; Robert Mittenthal, "Empires of Late," and from "Martyr Economy," Sprang Texts; Judy Radul, "Kisses So Wet"; Lisa Robertson, "Prologue" and "Eclogue I" from *XEclogue*, Tsunami Editions, and from *The Apothecary*, Tsunami Editions; Nancy Shaw, "Hair in a Knot," "In Doubt a Rose Is a Grotesque Thing," and "The Illusion Did Not Last" from *Scoptocratic*, ECW Press; Colin Smith, "Militant Tongue" and "Straw Man" from *Multiple Poses*, Tsunami Editions; Dorothy Trujillo Lusk, "Oral Tragedy," from *Redactive*, Talonbooks.

Introduction

Descriptions of the Kootenay School of Writing call to mind Voltaire's notorious summary of the Holy Roman Empire: "neither holy, nor Roman, nor an empire." For, indeed, few facts about this particular centre of avant-garde writing in Canada can be gleaned from its misleading name – it is not in the Kootenays, it is not a school, and it does not teach writing (at least, not in the ordinary sense).

Given such an ambiguous identity, the Kootenay School of Writing seems hardly the best place to orient oneself with respect to Canadian writing. Located in Vancouver in the extreme south-west corner of British Columbia, some six hundred kilometres from the actual Kootenays, KSW continues to find itself "misplaced" as far as mainstream Canadian literature is concerned. If one wants to learn special arts administration skills or leverage their cultural power and influence, the School would not be a wise choice for an apprenticeship. Its offices have always been small, the furniture used and in constant need of repair. Every address it has held has been low-rent and at a considerable distance from the city's better neighbourhoods, the last ten years on the 100 block of West Hastings, a street known across Canada for prostitution, pawn shops and drug use. In short, as an educational institution, KSW continues to be somewhat deficient in the day to day management of its operations. Yet for most of the writers and readers passing through its doors, it is precisely the school's deliberate failure as an institution that constitutes its unique cultural and literary value.

Throughout its existence, KSW's relationship with other writing institutions, especially those of high cultural repute and academic authority, has been one of mutual suspicion. Many of KSW's founding members, including Jeff Derksen, Gary Whitehead, Calvin Wharton and Colin Browne, sought not to establish a new professional elite, but instead denounced the very practice of canonising or somehow collecting certain writings or art pieces to form an exemplary aesthetics. KSW believed that cultural institutions that took pride in offering a well-organised administration centre usually forfeited concerns about art for an interest in management.

Where more traditional art institutions promoted ideas of cultural standards, KSW writers saw only cultural elitism. What motivated the school's formation was not a specific aesthetic vision, but rather a politicised understanding of how art and literary production often contributed to the ruling class's hegemonic influence over society. Mainstream culture had an important political role to fill. To writers working at KSW, most institutions of education and culture demonstrated little save the dominant class's privilege to determine aesthetic and moral principles within society. By contrast, the poetics of KSW emerged from the ruins of privilege, from a marginalised position in society that originated in language itself.

Strongly aware of the complex interdependence between art and ideology, KSW introduced to Vancouver, via workshops, readings and courses, their own highly politicised notion of writing. The school rejected the very idea that cultural value should derive from established canons or accepted traditions. To elevate a particular set of canonical writings above other works falsely supposed that art pieces somehow evaded or escaped their historical contexts to convey universal merit. The mainstream designation of a specifically "Canadian" masterpiece depended almost exclusively upon this contention – that true cultural value transcended material circumstances. Contrary to this view, writers working at KSW believed that what distinguished one canon of art from another proceeded mainly from the interests of whoever held capital and power. Resistance to an established canon, therefore, implied resistance to the social order that constructed it. To this end, they openly challenged any attempt by a socially dominant class to define specific aesthetic standards. To yield in one's writing to the master themes, tropes and voices of mainstream (Canadian) aesthetics was tantamount to relinquishing all control over the process of one's work. Indeed, the poets collected in this anthology rarely bothered with the dictates of traditional tastes; rather, they considered themselves to be writers whose primary objective was to maintain control over their writing, not just at the point of its creation, but its dissemination and, if possible, its reception as well.

Professionalism, with its attendant characteristics of good market sense and a penchant for self-promotion, meant little to most KSW writers. Of course, it is easy to romanticise this type of anti-commercialism within the vanguard as a type of deliberate, self-righteous scorn of the popular. Beat poets working at mid-century and many contemporary followers of "spoken word" tend to repudiate in their writing the entire institution of criticism, associating it with the twin evils of canon formation and class privilege. In Vancouver, however, in 1983, few established literary scenes of national attention actually existed. In fact, this is largely still the case. Most authority figures in the CanLit network developed their careers in either Toronto or Montreal. Hence mainstream taste in Vancouver's literary scene has not depended upon any distinct "official" school of thought or aesthetics.

If KSW writers rarely presented to the rest of Canada a bona fide movement, it was more due to their ongoing lack of resources than some deliberate refusal of formal organisation. No particular mode of writing or style of criticism evolved from the School, and, for this reason, it seems misleading to try to outline a genuine KSW aesthetics. Yet to read the writing that did develop in and around the small office quarters downtown is to perceive at times a strong communal identity based upon a shared approach towards class position and politics.

Inspired by labour unions and their capacity to effect significant social change, KSW often worked as well as wrote collectively. The prominence of collaborative work and thinking demonstrates the school's high regard for communal identities. In other words, what kept KSW writers together, either professionally or personally, was friendship and a common perspective on poetry. Attempts to formalise such relationships, whether through panel discussions, manifestos, or even simply review articles, usually failed since they could rarely capture the level of interaction that occurred outside the work itself.

Modernist doctrines of high culture, since their inception at the end of the eighteenth century, have continued to pursue a highly idealised sense of art as a discourse of moral value. According to such aesthetics, the motivating principle behind all cultural production remains social reform, as high art takes on the social role of a moral repository. Here culture not only preserves class rule, but also at times acts as a powerful tool of influence and even coercion. Historically much of the Canadian literary canon has followed this doctrine, with the moral imperative in modern art often increasing in intensity during times of political and social instability.

In its search for a politically relevant and class-conscious aesthetics, KSW rejected the didactic suppression of art forms in the service of civil reform – such as what recalls or might resemble socialist realism.

Accordingly, the school has often found itself criticised by both the left-labour community and various conservative members of society for not providing a more representative aesthetics of specific social needs. KSW, in its poetics and programming, has never directly sought out a particular community or cultural group (save perhaps those interested in writing), nor has the school attempted to build a new canon or representative literature. The school fosters no secret language or guiding moral and social doctrine among its writers. Rather its primary aim is to provide an open space where writers can develop and direct their own work outside all mainstream cultural institutions.

This is why KSW, when pressed for a profile, usually describes itself as a "writer-run centre." As both a workspace and a performance area, the school has traditionally organised itself at the point of production, i.e., at the point of writing, rather than according to some abstract social or aesthetic mandate. It is no accident that the house organ for the first ten years was simply called *Writing*. Here "writing" remains both the process and product, with the collective being responsible primarily for fund-raising and providing the necessary resources to permit both. Committed, in this way, to the practice of writing, KSW has garnered strong national and international recognition as a site of diverse, innovative activity. Its programming goals have always been aimed at providing local, national and international exposure to and for this particular community of writing.

What held KSW writers together has less to do with specific social ideals or shared notions of the communitarian good, than a critical sense of language itself as a prime constituent of community in general. In other words, community operates here as an effect of language, rather than the other way around, as more traditional writing and art scenes might assert. To define or even imagine a sense of community without proper consideration of the language used within it risked confusing shared social values with ideology. KSW writers spoke and worked together, but they rarely abstracted their work into specific doctrines or political manifestos. Instead what brought them together was an ongoing interest in discourse itself. Language, the practice of writing and the politics surrounding this practice have thus signified for KSW writers the very foundations of social interaction. To write is to engage in social discourse – an activity that is as culturally valuable as it is political.

II

Since its inception, KSW's programming has reflected an ongoing critique of canons and the ideological function of literary traditions. Its founding members were especially aware of the complex relationship between ideology and culture, acquiring some of their insight, and the inspiration to start KSW, after the provincial government shut down the Kootenay region liberal arts college, David Thompson University Centre.

Upon its re-election in the May 1983 British Columbia election, the Social Credit administration initiated a series of deep and pervasive cuts to government services. The ideology behind the cuts was known as "restraint," an effort to trim in order to eliminate what the party considered to be "unnecessary government." Bill Bennett's administration, along with the new budget, presented a "restraint program" consisting of no less than 26 bills to the legislature. When the scissors came to rest, Education was one of the hardest hit ministries. Class sizes increased, while in most schools the number of programmes decreased. In the case of David Thompson University Centre in Nelson, the entire college was given no choice but to close its doors permanently.

Given its progressive agenda and reputation for radical politics and art, DTUC must have seemed to the Socreds doubly threatening as both a hotbed of leftist thought and an important source of the decadent "liberal" excesses that had permeated education throughout the 1960s and 1970s. The immediate political context of these reactions can be located in the conservatism of the New Right just then obtaining power throughout the West. In fact, in one sense, one might interpret Socred legislation as simply the application of global economic structures to the British Columbia landscape. "Thatcherism," "Reaganomics," "trickle-down theory" and "voodoo economics" were some of the sobriquets applied to similar interventions originating in the US and Great Britain. As one group of intellectuals put it, "[l]ike many people in the province, we were shocked by the government's programme. As the weeks went by, what at first appeared a random assault on everything associated with liberalism and social democracy took on an insidious logic. It was a logic made familiar by Margaret Thatcher and Ronald Reagan: the brutal logic of the New Right."[1]

Thatcher came to power in May, 1979, while the "Reagan era" began fifteen months later in November, 1980. Hence, at the time of the Social Credit Party's re-election in BC in 1983, both of these earlier administrations of the New Right were already well established in their respective countries and had initiated profound changes at almost every level of society, including the cultural as well as the economic.

Like past Republican administrations, Reagan emphasised tax cuts for corporations and those in higher income brackets, less government assistance for social programmes, and increases in the military budget. For the most part, Thatcher's economic initiatives were similar, albeit with an added, much more aggressive focus on her country's strong trade union movement and massive social infrastructure. What was particular to Reagan's brand of conservatism was its dramatic sense of a moral crisis pervading American social relations, and the subsequent cultural initiatives thought necessary to address it. In other words, Reagan brought to the New Right a profoundly effective social sensibility, attacking the very psyche of his country as much as its economic policies. Commentaries on Reagan's sophisticated use of the media and adept rhetorical capabilities are numerous and well known. Whether or not one may agree with Reagan's ideology, few can doubt the incredible media presence and popularity he was able to command throughout his tenure. Little can be added here to the scholarship that already exists on the subject. Some analysis of Reagan's cultural message is relevant to this study, however, since much of its content closely parallels the rhetoric of the Social Credit Party, especially with respect to its "restraint" programme.

When Reagan took office in 1981, America possessed the strongest economy on the globe. Whether measured in tonnes of steel or number of cars produced or the quality of high-technology products, America led all other nations in production. Economically, the US had experienced massive growth for forty years, dating back to the beginning of World War II. What then constituted the source of the New Right's vision of socio-cultural crisis? Two oil crises in 1973 and 1979 respectively had severely challenged the US's most important industry and market, but on the eve of Reagan's inauguration, America was still running a global surplus in its foreign trade accounts, as it had every year since 1895.[2] Ironically, 1980 would be the last year the US exported more goods than it imported. By the end of Reagan's second term, America's cumulative trade deficit reached over 500 billion dollars, nearly 20 percent of the country's gross national product.[3] Nevertheless, Reagan's administration built itself upon the mostly symbolic demand for a stronger, deeper, more encompassing faith in American culture. Reagan's famous 1984 "It's morning in America" advertisement depicted a community of friends and neighbours who espoused homespun values. A new bride hugs her mother. An old man and a police officer hoist the flag in a schoolyard, while students pledge allegiance to it. The announcer proclaims that "America today is prouder, stronger, better; why would we want to return to where we were less than four short years ago?" There is no mention of Reagan's name in the TV ad, yet clearly he was popularly associated with a four-year period of moral rejuvenation – exactly the type of re-visioning of society with which BC's Socreds aligned themselves at the same time.

And where was America in 1980 morally or spiritually? As we've seen, the US was not experiencing the type of economic problems BC was in 1983. At the end of the Carter administration, however, fewer than 20 percent of Americans thought their country was politically or culturally healthy; 72 percent thought it was in disarray.[4] Inflation, at over 12 percent in 1980, was judged to be a primary cause of the chaos. Yet more significantly, it was the general future of American culture that harboured the real source of disappointment. Despite its healthy status among all other nation-states at the beginning of the 1980s, the US, its citizens believed, held disheartening future prospects. Throughout the country, for the first time in the postwar period, a substantial number of Americans began to worry about declining living standards and their quality of life. Quite unexpectedly, the American dream turned out to be exactly that – more dream than reality.

Such cultural pessimism can be traced to specific historical events. From 1968 to 1980, each subsequent administration seemed irreparably marred by both domestic and international crises. Johnson's and Nixon's respective terms had been damaged by the Vietnam War. Nixon ended his first term with strict wage and price controls in an effort to contain a 4 percent inflation rate. His second term finished prematurely in the face of the threat of impeachment by Congress. In October, 1973, less than a year before Nixon's resignation, the Organisation of Petroleum Exporting Countries (OPEC) imposed its first oil embargo on the US, causing gasoline and heating prices to double overnight. The Middle East provided a critical focus for the Carter administration as well, after militant Moslems in Tehran seized the US embassy there, holding its personnel hostage for 444 days.

These political events certainly threatened the US economy and its status in the world. Yet at another important level, the Middle East crises deeply affected the American sensibility, painting the entire decade of the 1970s as one permissive slide into moral degradation. Considered in tandem with the US's ongoing political turbulence, the social and cultural climate of the country seemed increasingly traumatic to much of the polity. Polls conducted at the beginning of Reagan's administration revealed that two out of three Americans considered themselves anxious about the political and cultural directions in which their country seemed to be headed.[5] Moreover, rather than interpret these changes as rooted in larger shifts within the political economy, those polled generally viewed the gradual rise in economic inflation and the corresponding decline in living standards as a moral problem. If America was in serious degeneration, the chief cause lay in its lack of ethical integrity and general failure to maintain a strong cultural constitution – not the rise in global oil prices or the costly defeat of its forces in Vietnam.

Into this sense of moral panic strode Reagan extolling a new vision of civic value. His rhetoric emphasised the restoration of the family, the neighbourhood, the community and the work place as vital alternatives against ever-expanding federal power. According to surveys taken for the Reagan campaign, a full 70 per cent of voters agreed with the Republican message that the right moral and social leader could rejuvenate the entire country. Confronting after the 1960s and 1970s what they labelled a demoralised, moribund "liberal" establishment, the new conservatism found ready public support for a social agenda based on discipline, ethics, property and traditional family roles. They countered pluralistic attitudes towards sexuality with a puritanical vision of self-control and moral rectitude.

Reagan's appeal for ethical leadership struck a chord within Canadians in the 1980s as well. The conservative agenda at this time was clear and unremitting: repent now. Only a return to more traditional cultural structures could faithfully address the current social degradation of the West. Like Reagan, the Socreds effectively announced a crisis situation within the BC "everyday." A new class struggle had been initiated, complete with new terms of exclusion and evaluation.

Throughout most of the postwar period, BC proved itself to be a wealthy, socially stable province that required little industrial diversification. Its plentiful supply of raw pulp and mineral resources, combined with the hydro-electric resources to process them, ensured ready employment throughout its territory. As the recession of the 1980s worsened, however, resource-based economies like BC were hit harder than manufacturing-oriented ones. For BC's conservatives, the economic need to diversify was never more apparent. The conservative political vision, accordingly, centred upon removing obstacles to developing a more solid manufacturing stratum within the province. Rhetorically, the Socreds expressed this vision as the development of a more favourable climate for investment. Within the tourism industry, the term climate had always been a particularly evocative selling point for the province. If the pleasant mildness of BC's coastal weather could be somehow identified with the province's financial health, a new influx of foreign investment might be attracted to its economy.

In practice, the reform of BC's economic infrastructure was anything but mild. In the US and in Great Britain, conservative politics in the 1980s centred upon policies of corporate downsizing and the restriction of federal powers. Deciding that previous administrative support for the "welfare state," with its attendant policies of government subsidy, was preventing economic growth, both Reagan's Republican administration and Thatcher's Tories studied the growing service sectors of their respective economies and set about the massive privatisation of their entire resource and manufacturing infrastructures.

Soon after their 1983 re-election, the Socreds wasted little time in identifying themselves as BC's official branch of the Thatcher-Reagan axis. In particular, Reagan's voice of moral concern and political crisis, Bennett found, could be easily appropriated for the situation in BC. The source of anxiety and the approaching social apocalypse, for Bennett, lay in the economic recession that had been worsening throughout Canada since the latter part of the 1970s. By 1983, BC unemployment topped 11 per cent, a rate not seen since the 1930s. Industry everywhere across the province appeared to be in decline, as foreign demand for its wood and pulp resources fell off. The BC legislature subsequently demanded new restrictions on expenditure in an attempt to consolidate its losses. "Restraint" and discipline, the Socreds argued, was the only course of action that could regulate such a dangerously unstable economy.

Describing previous administrations, including, presumably, their own, as bloated bureaucracies with excessive, decadent budgets, the Socreds immediately set about reducing government spending. New laws were proposed in the summer of 1983 as part of the "restraint" package to facilitate the mass lay-off of public workers and the de-regulation of certain social services such as employment standards, tenancy arrangements, and consumer rights. Within months, Bennett had restructured the entire public sector.

According to the Socreds, the critical state of BC's foreign markets demanded such drastic cuts in social spending. The size of previous governments had not only hampered the province's ability to compete in the new global markets, it constituted a threat to human individuality itself. Just as government would now need to purge itself of its past excesses, so too was the BC citizen called to re-affirm his or her dignity as an individual by relying less on public handouts. The policies of the New Right carried a particular psychological agenda, summarised as follows:

> There is a crisis: something must be done. And there is a voice within us that tells us to slash at the comforts we have accumulated, to attack those who have not yet suffered enough from the new order, to purge ourselves of the rot within. How can we deserve recovery unless we suffer the pain of restraint? There is no easy answer to this, except to say that sado-masochism is no more healthy in public life than it is in private.[6]

The strong, ethical imperatives in Bennett's agenda seem to have been lifted directly from Reagan's and Thatcher's earlier platforms. While the official rhetoric of Bennett's administration emphasised the need to create "a favoured investment environment," this objective was to be achieved only partially through fiscal policy. Much of the responsibility for rebuilding the province lay in the individual citizen. In addition to increased self-reliance in economic matters, the Socreds argued for a more puritanical sexual code and stronger family relations led by a return to traditional motherly and fatherly roles for men and women.

Projecting their desire for ideological and psychological purgation onto the economy, the new conservatism pursued a strict anti-statist policy, charging that the state bureaucracy which claims to mitigate the problems of unemployment, poverty, crime, etc., actually causes them by disturbing the "normal" function of the market mechanism. With its "tax and spend" attitude, the liberal state was sabotaging economic growth. Left to itself, the market would take care of the economy. With respect to cultural economics, this sensibility would help rationalise the type of cuts to arts funding the Socreds claimed were necessary. Only the private market was truly qualified to evaluate whether or not a particular art practice was worthy. If culture were to survive and prosper, it would have to be the consumer who ultimately decided what best represented a community's needs.

This essential faith in the capitalist system to function best with as little human interference as possible remains a core principle of conservative ideologies. Reagan intoned it, as did Thatcher, allowing them to rationalise cuts to social services as a form of economic and political liberation. The welfare state, they claimed, only limited true human capability by constraining economic growth through needless bureaucracy.

Bennett proclaimed similar views. Extolling their faith in the market norms, the Socreds sought to preserve capital's autonomy and, hence, its continued growth according to its own terms and values. Such claims on behalf of the supremacy of the free market rarely made any reference to class interests. Instead, this new conservative agenda emphasised a wider political ontology in which society functioned as an innately holistic structure, one best left to its own devices. In this context, "restraint" implied a type of altruistic sacrifice for the communitarian good, not just a specific privileged class. South of the border, Reagan would continue to present himself as a man of the people. In Reagan's America, privilege itself had become rationalised as a common good. Economic reform translated literally into a universal sense of cultural improvement, a value respected by the left as much as by the right.

Of course, even such radical moralism has limited influence when economic measures seem unjustifiably severe. Upon introducing their budget on 7 July 1983, the Socreds managed initially to aggravate every contingent of the left. In British Columbia, there seemed few options; and people did what people everywhere do when they are pushed too far: they took to the streets. Protest groups representing a wide range of communities and political positions formed the Solidarity Coalition to co-ordinate protests throughout the province against the budget and its attendant attack on human rights. Organised labour soon joined the fray by forming Operation Solidarity to protest the erosion of its own bargaining power. The two organisations were never quite at ease with each other, but given the equal threat to trade union practices and social rights, a practical coalition could be forged. Operation Solidarity announced itself only one week after the legislative package was introduced, and included representatives from virtually all of the province's unions as well as members from over 150 different activist groups. Its spokesman was Art Kube, head of the British Columbia Federation of Labour. Under Kube a series of rallies involving tens of thousands of people took place, climaxing in a one of the largest gatherings in the province's history at Empire Stadium on 18 July. A province-wide general strike became a palpable possibility.

However, as Bryan D. Palmer points out in his account of the events of 1983, many of the core objectives informing this oppositional front, while militantly pursued, were not radical in that they did not seek to topple BC's political economy. Operation Solidarity, it seemed to Palmer, was formed more to preserve social institutions than dismantle them. It was the Socreds, in this scenario, who were positioned as the real threat to the communitarian good, not labour. Accordingly, both the right and left often expressed the same general position with respect to the state and the current political system defining it: that it should be preserved and improved at all cost. The chief difference between the ideologies lay in what they identified to be the source of danger. Each side conceded that the political economy needed serious correction; where they disagreed was which areas of the province were secure and healthy and which ones required discipline.

Given this lack of genuine opposition within liberal culture, it is not surprising that conventional leftist coalitions found themselves criticised by more radical contingents as reformist and ineffectual. When the unions, under International Woodworkers of America leader Jack Munro, attempted to settle with the government, they were accused of selling out the intellectuals (teachers, students and activists), non-unionised workers and the unemployed in order to maintain the trade union's historical compromise with capital. On the eve of an impending general strike, the unions pulled their support in exchange for a government promise to review their legislative package, and to drop some of the more contentious anti-labour changes. With the general strike at least temporarily averted, the Socred agenda could be maintained. Deals like that, Palmer points out, run the risk of painting any conventional labour movement as little more than a "reformist bureaucracy [that] carved up the class struggle into its economic (trade union) and political (electoral) halves, imposed a trade union movement, and accommodated itself to the institutions and legalistic core of state policy in the emerging collective bargaining system of post-war North America."[7] For the radical opposition, such moderation is always viewed with suspicion. The reformist confusion of privilege with moral health effectively eliminates any possibility of a revolutionary class position being organised and launched against capitalist coercion.

Like most liberal or left-leaning institutions of education and culture in BC, DTUC quickly learned the significant role class structure played in the harsh politics of Socred economic reform. Located in the small eastern BC city of Nelson, DTUC drew its student population mainly from the large blue-collar community surrounding the area. The city itself had long been an important industrial centre in BC, and though the log booms and silver mines of the past were long diminished, it still supported an active working-class culture, much of it supported by BC's ever-important wood industries. Its many civil service offices confirmed Nelson's importance as an administrative and commercial centre. If you had to go to court in the Kootenays you had to come to Nelson. Even the RCMP substation was in Nelson. The place was full of old stone buildings dating back to the turn of the century, most designed by Francis Rattenbury, the architect who drew up the plans for the the provincial legislature and many of Victoria's municipal edifices.

Most importantly, throughout the postwar period, Nelson remained a heavily unionised town. Even in the 1980s its many sawmills and railyards continued to be unionised. Union logging truck drivers hauled union-cut timber right down main street through the middle of town, past the Chinese restaurants and the granite blocks housing the region's civil service centres. Visitors to Nelson would be hard pressed, for this reason, to find many Social Credit supporters. The political affiliations of the city were mostly left-wing, with a few edging towards some of the extreme fringes of the ideological spectrum. In the late 1960s and early 1970s, such a political climate drew many American counter-culture activists and Vietnam War resisters to the city, which in turn affected its political demographics. Hence, despite its small population of only 15,000 people, Nelson supported a surprisingly wide variety of eccentric, highly original communities and scenes. Hippie draft dodgers routinely shared the sidewalks with Russian speaking Doukhobors – the latter, a group of radical spiritualists who had left Russia in the nineteenth century to pursue their own utopia in the new world. Inspired by the promise of the western frontier, these "spirit wrestlers," as they called themselves, had travelled by way of the prairies in search of a life of peaceful toil. They shared with the American draft dodgers a strong anti-materialism, though they were more disposed to violent, revolutionary acts.

Every so often when the desire for earthly wealth got out of hand the radical Doukhobor Sons of Freedom sect might bomb the tracks or the power transmission lines or burn down a house (one of their own) that sported a television antenna. Only fire could purify the contaminating influence of western materialism.

Other purification rituals, performed by far less radical contingents of Nelson society, included the routine police incineration of marijuana crops after a particularly big drug bust. The Kootenays continue to be an important source for this agricultural product. As expected, the various counter-cultural groups populating this area kept the RCMP relatively busy. Indeed, throughout the 1970s and early 1980s Nelson became a prominent mecca for such activities, attracting more than its fair share of artists, musicians, actors and writers. At the start of the 1980s, most of Canada's more radical intellectuals had at least heard of Nelson, if not actually visited the city. Several of DTUC's instructors, such as Fred Wah, made a point of returning to teach there after living in other more cosmopolitan centres like Vancouver. They, in turn, were able to attract a steady supply of writers and artists eager to meet and interact with the city's varied cultural groups and networks.

Opening in 1978, David Thompson University Centre quickly became the intellectual centre of Nelson. Not only did it provide teaching opportunities for writers like Wah, Tom Wayman, David McFadden, John Newlove and Colin Browne, it gave students from the interior the occasion to receive their post-secondary education without having to move to Vancouver, Victoria or up north to Prince George. Combined with the city's dynamic cultural context, DTUC presented an almost ideal institutional setting for any students or teachers interested in less conventional approaches to art and writing. Although it could not grant actual university degrees, it did provide its own two-year writing diploma complete with university transfer courses underwritten by the

University of Victoria. There was even an independent writing journal, the aforementioned *Writing*, founded in 1981, to publish and distribute the new work being produced there. McFadden was *Writing*'s first editor, followed by Newlove in 1982. The magazine would survive the school's move to Vancouver, coming under the editorship of Nancy Shaw and Derksen, and was just as essential there as it was in Nelson.

As the 1980s began, the immediate social potential of this school seemed practically limitless. Centred prominently within a politically active, culturally exciting environment, far from the official eyes of Ministry of Education bureaucrats, DTUC was able to pursue a much more progressive pedagogy than other mainstream post-secondary institutions. Its approaches to teaching and education extolled an image of innovation as well as autonomy across the country. Identifying with neither conventional colleges nor large city campuses, DTUC prided itself on its fierce, almost anti-institutional independence in programming. Such a counter-cultural attitude, as we've seen, fits in well with the general political heritage of this area of BC.

Throughout the 1960s, 70s and 80s Nelson continued to attract a significant contingent of leftist intellectuals and avant-garde writers and artists. Both Newlove and Wah, like many other Western Canadian writers, taught in Vancouver at the University of British Columbia after getting their degrees there, but they would eventually return to the interior. This is not to suggest that the university disappointed Newlove's or Wah's literary aims. Far from it. At the University of British Columbia, almost twenty years before the founding of DTUC, they became part of a group of aspiring writers collected around the theorist and critic Warren Tallman. Tallman was an important figure in the more experimental writing circles in Canada, especially on the West Coast, as he had worked closely with many prominent poets in the US throughout the 1950s. He and Donald Allen co-edited *The Poetics of the New American*

Poetry, a companion volume to Allen's important 1960 anthology, *The New American Poetry*, which introduced writers like Allen Ginsberg, Charles Olson, Frank O'Hara and others to a broad readership. *The Poetics of the New American Poetry* investigated new strands of counter-cultural and avant-garde writing then being practised south of the border. Thanks to Tallman, these students encountered, years before any other city in Canada, some of the most current aesthetic theories and poetry movements of the US. By the end of the 1950s, the west coast in general featured a host of new centres and communities of innovative writers and artists. San Francisco was already billing itself as a leading site of counter-cultural activity. The publication of Allen Ginsberg's *Howl and Other Poems* in 1956 established the city as the capital of the Beat movement – especially after its publisher, Lawrence Ferlinghetti, was arrested for printing obscene material. Ferlinghetti's City Lights Bookshop and the Pocket Poet Series he published there became an almost overnight cultural sensation, attracting many would-be poets, bohemians and other cultural nomads to the Bay area.

The same year that "Howl" appeared in all of its notoriety, the experimental art school Black Mountain College formally closed its doors in North Carolina, sending even more avant-garde writers and artists westwards. For the poet Robert Duncan and his partner, the painter Jess, the loss of Black Mountain demanded an immediate return to San Francisco where they were most likely to find support for their work. Once there, Duncan wasted little time in organising special events and different reading series to introduce to the city some of the work and thinking Black Mountain had produced. Charles Olson, past rector of the college, revisited Berkeley at Duncan's request to deliver a five lecture series on history and the philosophy of Albert North Whitehead. Duncan's immediate circle of poets and artists, including Jack Spicer and Robin Blaser, became known as the "San Francisco

Renaissance"; and though not as widely recognised as the Beat Movement, these poets played prominent roles within the New American Poetry. By the late 1960s, at the height of the anti-war movement, the entire Bay area would be synonymous with American counterculture. Even a decade earlier, no other city in the US, save perhaps New York City, featured so many experimental scenes in writing and the arts.

Back in Vancouver, Warren Tallman, one of the most important early critics writing about the New American Poetry, had been both professionally and personally involved with this particular contingent of avant-garde writing right from its very beginnings. Few universities and art colleges outside of Berkeley in the West and Columbia in New York had yet discovered the experiments in writing percolating throughout the US's small presses and independent poetry magazines. Tallman taught in the English Department at the University of BC, and provided Wah, Newlove and a host of other younger writers who studied there with an invaluable mentor on the new writing. Not only was Tallman an experienced editor responsible for some of the first critical writings on the Berkeley and Black Mountain scenes, he remained in close contact with many core writers, including Olson, Duncan, Spicer, Blaser, Robert Creeley and Allen Ginsberg. Between 1959 and 1963, he brought Duncan up to Vancouver three times to engage with its writing scene. In 1963, along with Duncan, Olson and Ginsberg, he organized an important series of panels on poetry, epistemology and theories of writing. Two years later, Spicer joined Tallman at his house for a set of lectures and interviews on his own work. After San Francisco, Vancouver, it can be argued, was the primary port of call for experimental writers, especially those associated with the New American Poetry.

Surrounded by some of the most important poets of this movement, writers like Wah and Newlove became strongly influenced by their work. The Berkeley group, together with the Beats, presented Vancouver with a wide array of innovative strategies in poetry. After listening to Duncan in the early 1960s acclaim the importance of "little magazines" in new poetry movements, the younger Nelson poets, along with George Bowering from the Okanagan and Jamie Reid from Vancouver, were inspired to begin their own literary periodical – the anagrammatically named *Tish*. *Tish* helped organise the Vancouver writing scene as a new site of literary production. Once an official movement, the *Tish* group quickly established itself as the West Coast locus of avant-garde writing. As both a magazine and community of writers, *Tish* filled many functions in Vancouver. Operating foremost as an immediate record of new Vancouver writing, the periodical also strongly identified with the American literary tradition of the small, independent poetry journal. For example, Cid Corman's *Origin* and *Black Mountain Literary Review* as well as Leroi Jones's and Diane Di Prima's *The Floating Bear* provided important models for *Tish*'s format. *Tish* endured for eight years, publishing forty-five monthly poetry newsletters and a series of books and chapbooks.

In its content, *Tish* also followed the model of the small magazine at Black Mountain College. Duncan's and Olson's emphasis in their poetry on the local and physiological aspects of human experience seemed to *Tish* ideally suited to the college's modest, intimate, community-oriented publishing mandate. Wah and Bowering shared with Olson, Duncan, Spicer *et al.*, a profound suspicion of the lyric mode, rejecting its tendency towards symbolic abstraction. In Frank Davey's view, the poetics of Olson and Corman's *Origin* were a major inspiration behind *Tish*. *Origin* presented, for Davey, "not the usual aesthetic object but a field of force"[8] – what Olson described as "a REENACTMENT of the going reality of (approximate, shot at) THAT WHICH IS ABREAST OF US: now, here & now…"[9] *Tish* poets accepted Olson's repudiation of art as symbolic meaning, and promoted instead a poetry of "essentials." Consistent with its name, *Tish* kept its gaze downward towards the object and process immediately at hand. "No ideas but in things," wrote Williams almost half a century earlier, establishing what for *Tish* would remain the single most important credo for experimental poetry in North America. As Bowering points out in 1963, *Tish* poets literally "turned their attention upon the factual things that make up the world, men included among them."[10]

Many of the *Tish* writers later went on to teach in different universities and colleges across the country. In this aspect, they also followed the Black Mountain writers, for pedagogy had always been important to Olson's, Creeley's and Duncan's poetics. In the capacity of rector of Black Mountain College from 1948 to its closing in 1956, Olson worked as extensively on his pedagogy as he did in poetics. "It is not true," Olson wrote in 1954 defending his interest in education, "that, because of the increase of knowledge, it is no longer possible, or necessary that a man seek to master it all, all (François Rabelais, *e.g.*, was right, and is right, a man is the sum of it all, by whatever method he chooses, but with that as absolute end, or he is not worth our time)."[11] Indeed Olson rarely hid his own intentions to "master it all." His poetics, he believed, could provide the foundation for an entire new "stance to reality." Olson proposed outright that "the time has come for the men of knowledge to take over the task of making a NEW ENCYCLOPEDIA a level of attack and quality at least the equal of Diderot's."[12] Olson's encyclopaedia did not come to fruition; what should be emphasised, however, is Olson's critical interest throughout his career in reforming and revitalising American arts education to reflect a more creative, dynamic approach to knowledge in all disciplines, not just poetry. Poetics, for Olson, meant more than writing verse; to engage in poetry was to establish criteria for actual modes of perception. Running workshops and lecturing in San Francisco in the late 1950s as well as at various universities and colleges throughout the 1960s, Olson continued to stress the pedagogical as well as epistemological import of his writing. At the end of the 1960s, shortly before his death, he joined Creeley in establishing what is still today one of the most important post-secondary programmes in poetics and writing, the Buffalo Poetics Programme at State University New York, Buffalo.

The *Tish* poets may have possessed neither Olson's interest in epistemology nor his passion for institutional reform, yet many of them pursued some form of teaching position after finishing their own degrees. Bowering taught creative writing and English literature at several institutions, including the University of Calgary, Sir George Williams (later Concordia) and finally, returning to the Lower Mainland in 1971 to teach at Simon Fraser University (where his students would include a number of KSW writers). Wah and Newlove wasted no time in re-establishing themselves in Nelson where, now armed with their own poetics and a strong interest in pedagogy, they found work at the community college. When Notre Dame, one of the city's older catholic colleges, was sold to the provincial government by the Catholic Church for one dollar on the condition that it remain a university in perpetuity, these writers found ready support among Nelson's growing intelligentsia to renovate the building as a new, independent college for the arts. Here again, Black Mountain College provided an important model in this pursuit. Inspired by Olson's attempt to develop both a new poetics and a reformed pedagogy for the arts, Wah, Newlove and such recent additions to the staff as Colin Browne and Tom Wayman began offering short, intensive workshops in almost every area of writing, including poetry, prose, journalism and even script writing. As a result Nelson, long a refuge for various socially marginal groups, suddenly acquired the status of an internationally recognised centre for innovative teaching and writing. DTUC's name spread quickly throughout various writing communities across North America and soon the school was attracting well-known authors and artists for readings, book launches and extended workshops. Both Creeley and Duncan visited the school, as well as other Black Mountain alumni such as Fielding Dawson in 1980. Important Canadian writers, including Margaret Atwood, Michael Ondaatje, Brian Fawcett and Steve McCaffery, would also make appearances between 1980 and 1983. During its short five-year existence, DTUC followed closely both the structure and tradition of Black Mountain College, encouraging a new, younger generation of writers and artists to challenge mainstream ideas about art and politics.

When the Socred restraint policy was implemented after 1983 and financial cutbacks to the province's education programmes took effect, most DTUC students were quick to interpret such handlings as a direct attack on both their aesthetics and political positions. The history of Black Mountain College had impressed upon DTUC and the community surrounding it the ever-present possibility that progressive forms of art and writing could prompt hostility from conservative administrations. More than a difference in ideology, therefore, the Socred agenda represented to the DTUC community an entire cultural mood. To the writers, teachers and students working there, the New Right was synonymous with a new aesthetics – a new social sensibility, complete with revised terms of cultural support – or lack thereof. It was not sufficient to interpret the closure of DTUC as mere economic misfortune; rather, such decreases in funding translated into a fairly straightforward form of social exclusion.

III

Perhaps the most important example of this type of exclusion, at least in BC, can be seen in the formation of one particular front: the Industrial Workers of the World. In both its thoughts and activities, the IWW operated as a non-reformist, hence politically suspect contingent of workers. In BC especially, the IWW has historically constituted an important alternative to traditional labour politics. Anarcho-syndicalist in its orientation, the IWW, or Wobblies, as they were affectionately dubbed in Vancouver, once represented one of the largest unions in the province. Their influence surfaces still; and those in search of a less conciliatory opposition within the contingent coalition in 1983 became especially attracted to the political and cultural history of this movement. No analysis of the events of 1983 could be called thorough without some mention of the "Wobbly" sensibility as adopted by the more radical contingents of BC politics and aesthetics during the 1980s.

An important result of the events of 1983, as the Solidarity movement revealed, was the rise of class consciousness among intellectuals as well as workers. Class suddenly appeared radically re-drawn for many labourers, whether they worked with information or with bricks and mortar. The entire BC social strata appeared suddenly divided between "bad British Columbians," i.e., workers and intellectuals who refused to sacrifice for the communitarian good, and the worthy employing class, who continued to define just what the terms of this good would actually be. Those citizens who either directly or indirectly supported "restraint" announced themselves as a collusion of workers lacking class-consciousness, AKA scissorbills, labour skates and those unionists who continued to make their compromise with the values of liberal capitalism.

Given the growing perception that the Solidarity Coalition was a failure, the students at David Thompson University Centre, and in the creative writing programme in particular, also found it necessary to examine their class loyalties and assumptions. As the contingent coalition shifted in focus from a single-issue protest to concerns for an educational organisation, decisions were taken that could only come from heightened class-consciousness. Once in Vancouver, according to Jeff Derksen, the re-organised KSW even considered joining the Industrial Workers of the World. The actual decision to form or join a mixed local never progressed beyond the meeting table, yet the fact the overture took place at all is significant enough to indicate more than a passing familiarity with the Wobblies' history. From a radical perspective, the IWW had much to recommend it – especially during the time of Operation Solidarity. The Wobblies' brand of anarcho-syndicalism saw the general strike as the most important act in the overthrow of capitalism. And to settle for less than the eradication of this economic system would mean only defeat at the hands of the ruling class.

The IWW was historically strong in the Kootenays, organising more than 60 percent of the workers in Nelson at the turn of the century in its fight for the eight-hour day. In fact, it owes its very name to this area of BC; it was John Riordan, the Kootenay delegate to the IWW founding convention in Chicago in 1905, who insisted on the name Industrial Workers of the World instead of the Industrial Workers of America – an early example of Wobbly internationalism. It is also strangely fitting that in Vancouver in 1906 the Wobblies opened one of their first BC offices and reading rooms at 61 West Cordova, around the corner from the very block on Hastings that has housed KSW for the last ten years. This room had an extensive library of socialist material and speakers were brought in from all over.

An important source of structure for the Kootenay School of Writing can be traced to the IWW. From its very beginnings, its membership, consisting originally of Tom Wayman, Jeff Derksen, Gary Whitehead,

Calvin Wharton, Peter Cummings and Colin Browne, acted collectively. There were, and are, no leaders. Virtually all decisions are arrived at as a single body, an often cumbersome method that takes longer than any simple majority rules ballot box democracy. While its collective structure might not have been in conscious imitation of the IWW, both movements were organised as a concerted attack on hierarchy and privilege. Such principles, in turn, derived from a strong sense of class struggle and the valorisation of all workers' rights. One great thing about the working class is that you don't have to have a job to be a worker; the only thing you have to do is grasp the awareness that the working class and the employing class have nothing in common.

"Hammer," an early poem by Tom Wayman, who was also a Wobbly, illustrates the close relationship KSW maintained with labour movements. In it, Wayman symbolically abstracts the common tool of a carpenter – the hammer – into an emblem of social unity among the impoverished working classes. The image is hardly new, having signified basic labour in everything from Masonic badges to the flag of the Soviet Union. What is fresh in Wayman's poem is his descriptive prose, detailing the various working situations the hammer must transcend. In the final stanza,

> Nothing can stop it. The hammer has risen for centuries
> high as the eaves, over the town. In this age
> it has climbed to the moon
> but it does not cease rising everywhere each hour.
> And no one can say what it will drive
> if at last it comes down.[13]

Wayman's interest in class struggle is evident throughout the poem. All workers, regardless of their individual working situations, share an important social bond derived from their common oppression by capitalism. Class oppression and the need for social change it subsequently provokes unites, for Wayman, the restaurant cook with the carpenter, and both of them, oddly enough, with the astronaut. Labour does not ever cease in this poem; but neither does the need among labourers for emancipation and their social right to own the relations of production.

Only one year after KSW opened an office on West Broadway near Oak Street, the school co-sponsored, with the Vancouver Industrial Writers Union, a colloquium on what Wayman and others were calling "work writing." Among the issues discussed there was labour's unclear future within a Socred-administered province. Such political uncertainty generated a specific confusion regarding KSW's own relationship to conventional labour groups.

The problem with the labour movement by the mid 1980s for other KSW writers such as Derksen and Browne can be illustrated with reference to Wayman's poem, particularly, the last two lines: the fact that the speaker cannot determine when the hammer will fall or what it will strike points toward an ambiguous interpretation of class warfare. Every Wobbly knows exactly what the hammer will drive, and has no doubt that it will fall, if not today, then tomorrow: when the hammer comes down, it will drive capitalism from the face of the earth.

Other distinct political and aesthetic influences behind KSW's development appear in a variety of different art and writing movements outside the school itself. In particular, the work associated with the journal L=A=N=G=U=A=G=E, and Ron Silliman's essays on the "new sentence" provide important touchstones in the evolution of a KSW aesthetic. A full year before Tom Wayman's Split Shift Colloquium on new "work writing," an equally significant series of workshops under the banner of the New Poetics brought its own politicised engagement with language and art to the collective.

The New Poetics Colloquium ran for only three days in August 1985, yet its influence would be such that many of its themes and discussions would constitute core components of the school's aesthetics for the next decade and beyond. Most of the panels featured debates on political and cultural exclusion, explored in conjunction with different experimental approaches to poetry. The conference provided many KSW writers with what would prove to be their strongest aesthetic direction.

The majority of participants were loosely engaged with "language poetry," a writing practice known for its disjunctive, non-referential use of language. Emerging in the early 1970s, primarily in San Francisco, language, or "L=A=N=G=U=A=G=E," writing never defined itself as a formal school of poetry. Its most definitive critical statements probably appear in Silliman's essays on the "New Sentence." As an informal writing scene, however, it seemed to encapsulate best the work of many of the colloquium's speakers, most noticeably Charles Bernstein, Susan Howe, Bob Perelman, Lyn Hejinian, Barrett Watten, Carla Harryman, Bruce Andrews and Silliman himself. These writers provided fresh reflections on some of the more symbolic aspects of contemporary political violence and the complicated relationship language obviously had with ideology. The primary historical context for their work lay in the Viet Nam war, especially its representation in the American media. As one historian notes on the media's relationship to this war, no previous political crisis since the Great Depression had challenged the "reproduction of values, norms and actual behaviours" as broadly as this conflict had.[14] The symbolic effect of the war, as it was represented in the media, resulted in what many of these poets expressed as a severe cultural displacement, a banishment from the flow of symbolic production and information regardless of the medium in which it originated. The result, according to these writers, was an intense political scepticism that language could ever suppose itself neutral to ideological forces. Contradiction in ideology automatically presupposed contradiction and conflict in the modes of communication used within ideology. A key cultural response to this type of breakdown, Silliman noted, was an increased focus among writers on form and technique. Deprived of a stable community within which both writing and speech might actually be shared, the contemporary writer necessarily transferred his or her labour towards methodology. Poets subordinated concerns for expressive detail and lyrical ornament to more elementary ones for structure and procedure. In this task, the "language" writer follows closely the radical revisionary schemas of past modernists like Pound who thought it necessary to teach his audiences "How to Read," as evidenced in his primers, ABC of Reading (1934) and Guide to Kulcher (1970). In Silliman's words, evidence of a poem's value was once "predicated upon the image of the poem as individual craft of the artisan type, while now the collective literature of the community, an ensemble of 'scenes,' is gradually emerging as more vital than the production of single authors."[15] The efforts of Pound and other modernists to instruct their respective communities on how to read their work required a focus on methodology. For Silliman this parallel interest in how a poem was formally put together seemed even more essential among his own contemporaries. Not only did poets aware of the "discordance of contemporary life" need to instruct their audiences in method, many found it increasingly obligatory to construct the very audiences themselves. The production of poetry, according to Silliman, was tantamount to the constitution of a working community, independent of most consumer markets. Hence, the cultural exile Silliman and his colleagues had experienced during the Viet Nam war translated further for these poets into the deeper loss of their original social network, the final ruin within their society of any pretence to shared ideological codes and values.

Although the poetics of both the KSW and L=A=N=G=U=A=G=E offered strong critiques of consumer culture and the economics of capitalism that drove it, the writing movements experienced similar, often frustrating exclusions from conventional leftist and class audiences. When Pulp Press published *East of Main*, an anthology of poets living and writing in East Vancouver, many of the book's strongest criticisms came from the left, not the right, and the main target was the section dedicated to KSW writers. For example, Brian Fawcett, in his review of the anthology, reproved language writing (and, by extension, KSW work) for abandoning a more practical and communicative alliance with the labour movement.[16] Applauding language poetry's self-styled rejection of the more spiritual, expression-based verse of the Naropa school, Fawcett was quick to temper his comments with a firm critique of the confusing political ambiguity he found in their work.

Fawcett himself had been influenced, both politically and aesthetically, by many of the same postwar countercultural writers that influenced the Nelson group in the 1960s. At that time Fawcett's mentors included such refugees from the San Francisco scene as Stan Persky, Robin Blaser and George Stanley, as well as Tallman's *Tish* group. For these writers, much of the later work being produced at KSW in the 1980s seemed strikingly ambivalent towards the concerns and motives behind these earlier movements. Where the poetics of George Stanley might showcase explicit social commentary, or, in the case of Robin Blaser, an aesthetic celebration of individual creativity within mass culture, KSW held to few ethical principles outside the concerns and function of writing.

Again taking its cue from some of the tenets of anarcho-syndicalism, the Kootenay School of Writing organised itself at the point of production as opposed to that of reception. The school was rarely interested in showcasing established writers. Hence older countercultural activists and writers such as Fawcett continued to criticise KSW for its lack of fixed methodology and/or political stance. Without a more systematic strategy of cultural opposition, Fawcett felt, social relations could never be reformed effectively. Far from envisioning new cultural standards around which a series of institutional alliances might be built, KSW conceptualised instead a very different relationship to writing itself as both a process and ideological framework.

It is worth noting here that most KSW writers would likely have agreed with Fawcett's criticism, since social reform had never been the main interest of the collective. Given his position Fawcett was right to be critical of KSW aesthetics. As a writer of the New Left, he held a much more romantic vision of the artist's political exclusion from mainstream society. To experience cultural struggle and the marginalisation of serious art within popular markets, as both he and Blaser pointed out, was to confirm one's individualism.[17] By contrast, KSW never accepted any equivalence between social exclusion and individual autonomy within the state. To be politically disenfranchised did not automatically guarantee an objective perspective on social matters. The Kootenay School of Writing in its theory and practice has always been wary of the discourse of individualism for this very reason. Rather than signifying an artist's sovereignty from the constraints of capital, social exclusion signified to KSW writers little beyond class oppression. The Kootenay School of Writing has never claimed to be a visionary organisation in the leftist, or any other, ideological tradition. The school's primary political concerns focused instead on whether language, in art or writing, could effectively displace a system that works for the few at the expense of so many.

It is precisely this type of linguistic opposition to consumer culture at the level of language that gives Kevin Davies's "Pause Button" its radical class politics. Published in 1992, "Pause Button" presents language as a bona fide field of labour, much like any other mode of production. "Language" writer Bruce Andrews had developed similar ideas about poetic structure in his poem-as-field work. For Davies the critical situation most BC labourers found themselves in in the early 1980s meant that language too was at a turning point, since it played a role in labour relations. The very title of his book suggests both a cessation in production and in representation – it just depends on whether you have your media device in the playback or record function. Like labour in general, the very words in Davies's work seem somehow devalued or downsized. "The story," he writes towards the beginning,

> began to get tedious
> exactly at the moment of maximum frenzy. To
> load together lust-
> ful beasts – provoked to gnaw off
> what rot lifted up against un-
> equal faculties & extreme actions.[18]

Indeed, even the most sincere attempts at cultural reform tend to become tedious at the moment they confront danger, compromising their conflicts in the name of communal meaning. Davies pauses, or pushes the pause button, in the middle of his discourse, separating the syllable "un" from the word unequal, as if he were editing a particularly indiscreet message, severing the offensive syllable from the liberal principle (equality) it had somehow tarnished.

The relationship of language to labour, Davies reminds us, categorically invokes those terms of production necessary for culture to recover or satisfy its own constitutive ruptures. This is why in conventional poetics only language, the very tool of disintegration, is able to heal our cultural rifts. Here the traditional duty of the poet is to pause and to erase conflict, especially if s/he can't provide the principles of unity needed to restore social harmony. Davies may pause in "Pause Button," acknowledging the fractured state of the symbolic order, but he does not erase that which signals the debt. What spaces do exist throughout the poem are designated as such, bracketed off within the type, alerting the reader that something is, in fact, missing.

> Information-needy, 26. Seek [   ] for [   ]. Absolutely
> Pyjamaless. Check [   ]. Yank hair into place, thrust face
> Forward, hit [19]

Like most workers facing the first major recession of the post-war, information-based economy, the subject of this personal ad is "information-needy." Yet the object of his desire refuses to appear, even symbolically. Davies's language stubbornly refuses to provide compensation. If there is resolution in Davies's poem, it comes so violently: "Remove the rug, replace it with the floor, sit, pluck splinter, spit, / – & so got tromped on pretty / hard, stomped, made to feel silly, extra –."[20] The reader is not certain if the subject being beaten in the last line is the same one who placed the ambiguous classified advert, that is, whether the violence has been meted out culturally or economically, or both. Such distinctions seem hardly necessary in the language of "Pause Button." Davies's symbolism does not represent a fractured cultural order, it enacts it on the page as it is read.

Similarly, Gerald Creede's long poem "Résumé" details a subjectivity both symbolically and economically beaten:

> I wrote him
> He didn't write
> He wrote: now that lilacs are
> In bloom she has
> Explosives.
> He painted his apartment
> A shade called Fled Yellow
> His life a series of small deals that
> fell through.[21]

Both the "normal" functioning of the market and of discourse has failed the speaker. His letters receive no reply from, one presumes, prospective employers, maintaining a symbolic as well as economic debt. As with Davies's penchant for bracketed spaces, Creede's résumé inspires little faith that the symbolic void in discourse will be eventually filled. The résumé fails to resume. Creede's language actively disavows a speech in which the subject can articulate his or her position or agency. Instead, Creede, too, brackets off the disruption he sees within his culture, in an effort to construct his own class position autonomous from mainstream society. Creede's struggle begins in lieu of the résumé, in a cultural space between jobs, often on UI benefits with little hope, or even interest, that the state will respond: "I won't watch my mouth," Creede continues, "I won't make it with you."

In Dorothy Trujillo Lusk's work, it is not a specific genre that represents class struggle, but the structure of language itself producing its own distinct agencies through historical development. Lusk's "Oral Tragedy" samples literally dozens of different allusions and references to other works, re-structuring them to reflect a more immediate, less historically idealised sense of context. The results are both witty and provocative:

> You are left with what you get and
> Your love is dross
> Well you remain whose world is none of mine
> I who lov'st well remain left.[22]

Here Pound's famous passage from the *Pisan Cantos* – "what thou lov'st well remains" re-emerges, stripped of all heroisms and ethical imperatives. Once again, we as readers are forced to recognise the waste, the detritus, in contemporary language where not even Pound's popular summary escapes the effects of changing political contexts and subject positions. Conventional cultural patterns quickly break down. Lusk evokes a world that "is none of [hers]." More importantly Lusk specifically connects this quality of loss with ideological leftism: she who has loved, who has experienced cultural passion, seems condemned to a life on the political margins. Recalling Pound's political experiments with fascism, Lusk injects a note of irony in her reading of his work.

Rehearsing a comparable antagonism to mainstream culture some years after leaving KSW, founding member Jeff Derksen emphasises what he calls an "aesthetic rearticulary practice." Derksen's poetics, in his own words, attempts "to articulate links across discourses and fields in a dialogism that is aware of ideology and its effects."[23] Most importantly, Derksen seeks to avoid what he terms the "absorptive" dynamic of pluralism where political critique is compromised through a romantic sense of individual rights. Once again, rather than cultural reform, Derksen chooses as his objective, cultural "inform," *i.e.*, a critique specifically attuned to the nuances of ideology and its influence on culture. Because such nuances begin at the level of language, so, too, must their critique. Here language is re-situated, re-connected to the various political contexts in which it originated.

> "Jeanine is a living example of Noranda's attitude to employees."
> [...]
> "We may not have all the right answers, but we have the right car."[24]

At first these disjunctive lines may convey little sense either together or separately; yet looking closer at the words themselves invokes specific political questions about the language being used. For example, how are we as readers supposed to imagine "Jeanine" as "a living example"? Can individuals be living examples? The answer, according to Derksen, helps underline his entire poetics. When individuals feel alienated by their own language, they are nothing but examples. Every syntactic structure creates its own exemplary figures or objects. By highlighting the paradox in this relationship between individuals and language, Derksen neatly conveys the inherent political and cultural limits in all discourse. In a later essay, he describes his use of language as an explicit act of aggression, a "refusal to adopt broken tropes of representation, social facts torn from their backdrops and placed in uneasy irony next to other contradictory discourse, floating quotations, a refusal to cite sources, a disregard for literary qualities," and most of all, "a refusal to try and find an outside to ideology."[25] Positioned as such, ideology effectively resurfaces from its popular encasings within a cultural discourse of value. Stripped of their pretensions to a universal sense of the communal good, of all access through language to civic or cultural virtue, seemingly benign references to the everyday are reconfigured, in Derksen's work, as explicit ideological components. As with Davies and Creede, to move through Derksen's language is to explicate quite precisely the myriad interconnections between market structures and the symbolic organisation of social relations.

The poem "Interface," for example, at first glance appears to consist solely of a series of disjunctive sentences, mostly declarative, culled from a wide range of sources, including personal reflection, economic statistics, and news headlines. Aside from the slightly disorienting effect such writing has on the reader, a closer inspection reveals an intriguing set of inter-relationships between the political, the social and psychological.

> The translation process that ends with "harvesting
> The necks of the infidel aggressors."
> Pure desire arrives like a train – on rails[26]

On one level, in these lines, Derksen acknowledges the obvious social distance between acts of translation and those of public execution. Working for a book publisher in the late 1980s, Derksen himself likely experienced first hand some of the social contradictions inherent in publishing explicit politicised texts at the safe cultural distance usually befitting intellectuals. Certainly there is a sense of privilege in choosing to view class conflict symbolically as opposed to literally. Yet the contradiction made explicit in the language here expertly reveals just how central a role language plays in all areas of political conflict. Both the "harvesting" of necks and the linguistic process of translation are presented by Derksen as completely interdependent cultural activities. The very term "harvesting" implies a concept of cultivation equal to any other discursive event. Regardless of whether the objects of cultivation be human heads or foreign words, the symbolic act of harvesting remains closely associated here with basic social coercion. In the act of translation, Derksen suggests, a specific violence is being performed, a movement of cultural purification as controversial as any act of ethnic cleansing might be. Language as a form of symbolic power has always been central to the ideological structures within modern capitalism, a relation that few KSW writers take for granted; for them, class struggle begins at a linguistic level before other, more material strategies can even be contemplated.

Linguistic relations reveal further institutional ties in the work of Deanna Ferguson – specifically the institution of patriarchy. Unlike Derksen's paratactic socio-economic commentary, Ferguson's lines at first suggest a more continuous narrative:

> In using the telephone, she says, I really gave so-and-so
> a good reaming, reprimand city,
> Soon enough, circularities of story, intimacies shared.
> Bullshit made apparent, but
> What is constructed in this world
> Has at least a shelf-life.[27]

If there is contradiction in this work, it emerges at the level of syntax first. Ferguson does not clarify whether the adverbial clause "in using the telephone" modifies "she says" or "I really gave." In other words, is the subject using the telephone to give the other un-named conversant "a good reaming" or merely to tell she has done so? The logic of the narrative supports the latter meaning, for how could one make specific use of a telephone to reprimand a person, save as a device of communication; yet the syntax of the line suggests that in the actual use of the instrument, the reprimand was given. Similarly, the jargon "reprimand city" plays with two meanings, making a pun of her terminology. Even after closely considering the different sections in Ferguson's long poem "Wanke Cascade," from which the above is taken, the reader inevitably realises that s/he is no nearer to a sense of "shared" narrative than when s/he began. The point at which the description or representation of the supposed event actually begins is not clear here. Ferguson displays two fictions simultaneously, or rather two levels of a linked fiction: "circularities of story, intimacies shared. / Bullshit made apparent, but…" Once again, the medium of communication appears to disrupt more than it transmits.

What in the romantic poetry of social anger or in a "work poem" might appear as a literal complaint cannot overcome its discursive origins, and so retreats back below the linguistic surface. Only "fabrication remains intact"; and this, Ferguson implies, remains the real target of her critique. The poet, and a female poet especially, cannot simply escape her social role or create a new one; her language works against it. But the ideological forces affecting her diction do not necessarily mean that she is completely powerless. It is no small feat to recognise and acknowledge the conditions of one's exclusion. Exclusion carries with it its own shades of autonomy and possible freedoms. She concludes,

> until all events speak for themselves
> until representations know what it feels like
> until positioning in the order is located
> until orders of knowing suss up
> until strata is axed as metaphor
> until economic isn't always the organizer
> fear, baby.[27]

Such are the demands Ferguson makes, not only on her social condition, but on language itself. To revolt against the political economy of liberal capitalism is to abandon all of its cultural institutions, including those guiding communication and representation. Once again, as she suggests, exclusion from mainstream culture invokes its own terms of agency and capability ("fear, baby"). Ferguson is in charge of her language to the extent that she doesn't have to communicate, if she doesn't want to communicate. Perhaps the most cogent example of this form of cultural defiance is her refusal to participate in this anthology. It is difficult to assemble works from so many disparate writers, despite their similar origins and collective engagements, without risking reductive categorisations of a poetry that, by its nature, remains highly dependent upon context for much of its import and innovation. Ferguson is right to be wary of being included in such a project, and she wastes little time in demonstrating her obvious sense of exclusion even here.

Other significant political issues besides those usually associated with capital and class relations contributed to KSW's collective cultural stance. A vital feminist politics and gender-based position continues to inform much of the work being done there. In fact, for poets Lisa Robertson, Nancy Shaw and Catriona Strang, involvement with the Kootenay School of Writing demanded a redress of the disproportionate number of male writers who originally constituted the collective. If language, as Silliman argues, ultimately displays "a determinate coding passed down to us like all other products of civilization," then most common, everyday writing practices must contain influences of the patriarchy as well as those of class struggle. In Derksen's view, poetry functions ultimately as a means of unveiling these "determinate codings." Yet woman writers working in and around KSW quickly noticed that most efforts to explore ideology within the school's programming tended to subordinate gender issues to those of class. In their work, writers like Robertson and Strang imply that the collective, though politically aware of the economic bearings on writing and language, rarely referred to the patriarchy in either its programming or individual poetry projects. Hence a more explicit reference to the linguistic components of the patriarchy constitutes the poetry of the "The Giantesses," a contingent coalition that worked within KSW. The Giantesses wrote together from the late 1980s to the mid 1990s and included as core members Robertson and Strang as well as Christine Stewart and Susan Clark. Clark, born in BC, edits the influential poetry journal *Raddle Moon*, and provided the Giantesses with a medium to publish and disseminate their work. With a nod to the male-centred revisionary modernisms of the last century, these women offered a complex feminist investigation of language that began with their own manifesto.

A. WE HOLD THESE TRUTHS TO BE SELF-EVIDENT:

1. Dissensual language is a machine of enchantments.

2. This machine, with all its archaisms, is a means of locomotion toward polysexual futures.

3. Wrenched history is our machine's frontier.[28]

Reminiscent of some forgotten passage from the archives of Futurism, the Giantess manifesto described a type of exaggerated nationalism taken straight from the pages of the high modernist tradition. Such metaphors of statehood or nationalism extended to the very name of the Giantess collective. Declaring themselves "Barscheit Nation," they inaugurated their own frontiers in a loud, brazen experiment in political secession from the patriarchy. Part poetics, part social theory, Barscheit Nation modelled its structure almost entirely after a machine. Its logic was primarily technical, its vision brutally forthright, cold, determined – in other words, "self-evident." Such a construction, it might be argued, seems hardly suitable as a feminist critique of patriarchal culture, especially since both the language and format of this work recalls some of the most excessive strands of modernist, misogynist writing and thought. The celebration of the machine as a source of kinetic energy and social wonder seems more consistent with the writings of Wyndham Lewis or F.T. Marinetti than the literature of feminism.

Rather than evoking ideas of unlimited progress and the promise of technological advancement, however, the Barscheit "machine" is one of "enchantments" only. Here typical masculinist clichés about the machine and technological rationalism are effectively re-appropriated for Barscheit's own anarcho-feminist project. The fact that language intrinsically carries gendered messages has never seemed more explicit. Where older feminist strategies in literature and criticism traditionally employed intense psychologisms, combating masculinist emphases on materialism and empirical reason with a focus redirected towards interior states of being, Barscheit Nation engaged a more deliberate constructivism. The language of Barscheit Nation, suitable to their collective stance as "Giantesses," remained pure exaggeration. In this manner they not only challenged the misogynist derivations of high modernism, but the equally problematic search by conventional women writers for an essentially feminist language or mode of thought. The political and cultural movements of the modern patriarchy continue to celebrate the machine as a paradigm of efficiency and control and these are precisely the qualities The Giantesses seek to exploit in their own poetics.

Like the IWW, KSW has traditionally held that any form of institutionalisation, whether of labour or aesthetics, remains fundamentally in support of hegemony. Here one might recall that the IWW's political objective was not to reform capital, but overthrow it. In a similar fashion, KSW did not conceive itself as merely a new trade college. In tracing both the school's political stance and ideological critique to a specific history of leftist struggle in the 20th century, namely, anarcho-syndicalism, a consistent position begins to emerge amidst the myriad writing and theory projects that took place there over the past decade.

Unlike America in the late 1960s and early 1970s, BC in the 1980s was not engaged in any war. It would appear, nevertheless, that the strong cultural and social dissent associated with the Socreds at this time provoked a similar sense of cultural displacement among many of the members of the KSW. With the shutdown of DTUC, they experienced their own loss of a previously prominent social network. Newly branded as a source of unnecessary government spending, what was once an important independent post-secondary institute of learning suddenly found itself recast as a morally suspect, decadent waste of community effort. Culturally, that is, on a symbolic level, a new struggle had been initiated by the Socred political apparatus, forcing these writers to respond with a symbolic attack of their own. More than the organisation of pickets and rallies, the writers collected in this anthology saw it as necessary to investigate speech itself. This shift in political strategy firmly divided them from previous working class aesthetics, just as it continues to set them apart from mainstream culture. Their work is difficult, at times astonishingly so. But it is also pointed, funny, and, most of all, extremely relevant to its place and time. Silliman's theory of the New Sentence identified difficulty in writing with the building of a new community or scene. This congruence suits KSW well. Between 1984 and 1994 the drive for an alternate poetics fuelled corresponding aspirations for a new political critique and a distinct community formation. KSW succeeded on all fronts.

1 William K. Carroll, Warren Magnusson, Charles Doyle, Monika Langer, R.B.J. Walker, *The New Reality* (Vancouver: New Star Books, 1984), p. 13.

2 Steven Schlosstein, *The End of the American Century* (New York: Corydon Books, 1989), p 4.

3 Schlosstein, p 4.

4 Patrick H. Caddell, "Crisis of Confidence: Trapped in a Downward Spiral," *Public Opinion* October/November, 1979, p 5.

5 Connecticut Mutual Life, *Connecticut Mutual Life Report on American Values in the '80s: the Impact of Belief,* (Hartford, Connecticut: n.d.), pp 86-97.

6 Magnusson *et al.*, p 271.

7 Bryan D. Palmer, *Solidarity: The Rise and Fall of an Opposition in British Columbia* (Vancouver: New Star Books, 1987), p 25.

8 Frank Davey, "Introduction," *Tish No. 1-19* (Vancouver: Talon books, 1975), p 7.

9 Olson, "Letter to Corman," *Letters to Origin* (London: Cape Goliard, 1970), pp 10–11.

10 George Bowering, Editorial, *Tish* 20, 1963.

11 Letter to Carl Sauer, cited in Ralph Maud, *Charles Olson's Reading: A Biography* (Carbondale: Southern Illinois University Press, 1996), p. 102.

12 Charles Olson, "A Bibliography on America for Ed Dorn," *Collected Prose*, ed. Donald Allen and Benjamin Friedlander (Berkeley: University of California Press, 1997), p 307.

13 Tom Wayman, "Hammer," *Did I Miss Anything?* (Madeira Park, BC: Harbour Publishing, 1993).

14 Michael X. Deli Carpini, "US Media Coverage of the Vietnam Conflict in 1968," *The Vietnam Era*, ed. Michael Klein (London: Pluto Press, 1990), p 18.

15 Ron Silliman, *The New Sentence* (New York: Roof Books, 1978), p 61.

16 Brian Fawcett, "East Van Uber Alles," *Unusual Circumstances, Interesting Times* (Vancouver: New Star Books, 1991), pp 91–102.

17 See for example Robin Blaser's essay "The Violets: Charles Olson and Alfred North Whitehead," *Line* 2 (Fall 1983), pp 61-103.

18 Davies, *Pause Button* (Vancouver: Tsunami Editions, 1992), p 9.

19 Davies, p 8.

20 Davies, p 8.

21 Gerald Creede, "Résumé," *Ambit* (Vancouver: Tsunami Editions, 1993), pp. 18-26.

22 Dorothy Trujillo Lusk, "Oral Tragedy," *Redactive* (Vancouver: Talonbooks, 1990), pp 11.

23 Jeff Derksen, "Disgust and Overdetermination," *Open Letter* 10:1 (Winter, 1998), p 9.

24 Jeff Derksen, "Interface," *Dwell* (Vancouver: Talonbooks, 1993), pp 8, 9.

25 Derksen, "Disgust and Overdetermination," pp 9–10.

26 Derksen, "Interface," p 5.

27 Deanna Ferguson, "Wanke Cascade," *The Relative Minor* (Vancouver: Tsunami Editions, 1993), p 19

28 Ferguson, p 19.

29 Lisa Robertson, Nancy Shaw and Christine Stewart, *The Barscheit Horse* (Toronto: The Berkeley Horse, 1993) (unpaginated).

GERALD CREEDE

Résumé

I wrote him
He didn't write
He wrote: Now that lilacs are
in bloom she has
explosives.
He painted his
apartment
a shade called Fled Yellow
His life a series of small
deals that
fell through
I burned my
bridges while they were still
in the erector set while father read the instruction
sheet
My life a series
of small deeds
that fell
through.
He thought the bugs
on the window were birds
outside it.
I wrote,
The rich fancy themselves
lions, but lions don't horde
the rich store,
chipmunks have the same courage.

It must have rained
I see
a dorsal
at my window
sill
that chick is shake of ship in placid
so facile the tone of the sheen amazes me
the char leases a shard leans, pleases
cease ill needle mender spent
dentless, dour hourglass
flinch grounder bounces resolute
& hidden, unbidden, unbespoken
bounder from a bent squealer
music flows oddly & otherwi
appeases block in middle
green loads lob the words
in rim shots, paragraphs on high
hat! the strain of string
the irony in packages
cavalier in unresponsive
dunces! time packages lode passages.
Let me walk
the seawall
one more
time.

   I wrote her and she didn't write me, if it's like the gleaning
of your own memory, like, then you know what she's really
like, she's like you,
Like as to make our appetites more keen
   so why the want of more detail, ponderings, you vain you.

I worked for Charles Laue Ltd., a brake part manufacturer, where I was employed as a quality control inspector. I gained experience with micrometers, rules, shadowgraphs, and other precision measuring tools.
squirrels
store
nuts
their estates
palatial
I beg your
rose garden I never
promised you a
hardon.

The cools are in an outroar & the pallans rage inright. The shmoahs refute any connection to their calumbinds, and the shesharsee disconnect all literal ramifications and put the din-dus on the shmoahs. The shmoos accept then fake the blame, own the puntahs on relays, growlifications, hick diggens. At this jincture Wilbur defected to the shomoolies, stabbed in the abacus.
Then knighted
by Charles III
and allowed to
usurp the present Duke
of Buckingham.

I whirled, whirling
into her arms
her mouth tasted
of scotch & tea
she was a woman
of the last few
centuries.

genius chisels
& the living die

I won't watch my mouth
I won't make it with you

lettuce
tomato
doesn't
may amaze!

hilk
dilgens

I was employed by Wesgar Industries, a sheet metal shop
which formed and cut panels for computer hardware assem-
bly. I gained experience in all stages of sheet metal set up,
shearing, forming, drill press, and learned the use of basic
measuring tools and gauges.

She wrote. I hear the creaking in the winter night, wire
spun through slender fingers, talking in the cold off the line,
snapping pins on apron waistbands. When I'm walking, he
says, I hate cars, but when I'm driving, he laughs, I hate pedes-
trians, explaining how life is. Equivicator.
one, two, ted, four.

I got the blues so
bad she didn't
leave me
– She was gone.
Even the plant she
left grew
away the plank
we shared
walked off.

That our
enemies
are our
friends in dream
is no mistake
neither that our
friends lie
there.
To choose the wrong
door is a mistake
but it's not
a mistake
in dream
to choose the wrong door.

He wrote:
when you fail
we'll still have
each other,
come
telling
in
pense

Next
to him
was as
close
as I
got

I don't
want to
remember
this like
it was
yesterday

They were
all in a row
the points made
in order and
useless to
highlight or
understand

I asked her maybe
to see what I miss

   Are you accepting job résumés, I asked the receptionist
who reached I thought at first to push the button summoning
security, but only into the desk for an application.

A landscape of the north shore. Fancied flames in the fore
that don't look real, an inspired mix of black and shades of
gray, a little yellow, blue buried in back, a podge of pink, red,
mauve, yellow and bum brown crumpled and flushed, yellow
and orange made red by two dark shades of blue, a pink one
called what? they were at the beach it and I enveloped, the
palm trees started out beach umbrellas. A tight white
colour everyone
in the
waiting room were
crippled they admitted
it even the
doctors.

while machines rest they fix themselves

There is
no infidelity
in dream
if there
were it wouldn't
be called
dream
like minds
that don't
need all
the detail
like

catapult the partialist

derelectics

if 5 were 3

I hear voices but
I'm always listening to something
else
and miss
what they say?

Vancouver looks like Malta used to.

There's no other
place around the place
so this must be the
place I reckon.

    Education: Lined up, sleeve rolled,
        for inoculation.

… jo blocks, torque wrenches, rivet guns, stop watches. I am
familiar with small warehouse procedures and assembly plant
operation.

He wrote:
If she didn't
wet the seat
I've nothing
to drink.

    The room was airy so I sat alone in the corner of it while
my financial records, my search for income, was questioned in
a manner the tone implying I had a yacht hidden away some-
where. I kicked my deck shoes under the corner of the desk. "I
didn't come here to jump on no Welfare Bandwagon," I
pleaded, "I need retraining."

I think: workshop it if you want, and then
sit on it for about a month. It is a *résumé*.
Did you leave anything out that ought to be
in? (Me, I wouldn't know…)

I walked 37 miles with my shoes tied
Got a paisley print on my necktie
Got a King James Version at my bedside
Covered in weathered cow hide.

December 17, couldn't sleep, reindeer on the roof.

the lights on the dock
are just like the ball
park
      cables rise into the
dark
      like home runs

KEVIN DAVIES

from Pause Button

[

– {yellow}   {flowers}
{& mingle more}

{incomplete}   {enough to}   {force}   {weather}

{to}
{*do*}
{you}

{possible}   {government}   {surveillance}

{miserable}   {exile}   {guards}   {public}   {rooms}

{a blank}
{roasted}
{newspaper}

{Electricity yet}
{dog-eared}

{shrill}   {tobogganists go down}   {landscape}

{reminiscent}   {chronology}   {response}
{in time for}   {space}

{the}
{fiery}
{subway}
{silence}

{elliptical}   {repression}

{rational}   {tattoo breeze}

{gathered}   {bourgeois}   {wool}

{life}
{haunts}
{training}

{images}
{behaving}

{edit}   {personal}   {disguise}

{primers}
{are}
{possible}
{blisters}

{cold}   {computer}   {consulate}

{meaning}   {of}   {production}

{unbelievable}   {drunk}   {dream}

{building}   {a great}   {years ago}   {doubt}

{a}
{direct hit}

{to the satellite}
{vibes}

{sharp}   {inadequate}

{crushed}
{murmur}

{verbal}
{rivet}

{for}   {ever}

{a simple}   {demonstration}   {element}

{held}
{against}
{us}

{petrified}   {specialist}

{intelligible}   {bondage}   {connection}

{bungled}
{brevity}

{sophisticated}
{impossibilist}
{stabbed}
{vegetal}

{hydrant}

{giving} {more} {clerk} {fuzz}

{nonswimming} {nonphosphorescent} {border} {notes}

{from which}
{burst}
{psychological arms}

{the most}
{mid-fuck}
{alley}
{cult}
{logics}

{I guess you all know}
{Gerald}
{Stumbling-Upon-Graveyard's}
{adolescence}

{civilization's} {pretty-nice} {late-night} {Pompeii}

{voted}
{best}
{municipal}
{pleasure}

{the thirty-five-word}
{work-hour}
{yonder-continent}

{if} {male} {impulse} {make} {malls}

{vagrant} {voices} {snap} {back}

{mental}
{duty}
{over}
{mud}
{pamphlet}

{demonized} {in-house} {vengeance} {feature}

{the}
{published}
{future}

{a lust for} {dictation}

{numb}
{ticks}
{transfixed}
{upon}
{jagged}
{alien}

{counter-masturbatory}
{above}
{unsatisfied}
{trash-gardens}

{shells} {follow} {function}

{capital} {machine'd} {bungling} {bulging}

{any}
{TILTED}
{vibrating}
{rowhouse}

{abstract} {people} {work-to-do}

{gravity}
{is}
{historical}

{project} {dim} {coercion}

{shackled} {sugar} {attention}

{with chalk we}
{think}
{the record}

{sexed}
{out loud}

{horse-betting} {philosopher} {rereads} {grasses}

{welfare}
{good for}
{asthma}

{bits of me}
{are mighty}
{thong}
{paste, to}
{travel along}
{smack & plastique}
{in the Queen's bags}

{pumping}　{in the}　{back}　{water}

{earnings}　{&}　{lubricated}　{id}　{twitching}

{little}
{plant-anima}
{with a}　{name}

{the roof}　{fell in}

{buying}　{unbroken}　{gestures}

{flipped}
{coin is}
{form}
sucking

LARY TIMEWELL

from Ruck

Well met, antipathy! Diaphanous
garment-condition of work, little
violin d'Ingres of semi-retired, tight-lipped facsimiles.

Drone mogul endures, tangential to
theory's impossibly patristic squat,
the confident suffrage of our little dog Doxy.

Seep patrician grousing.
Equipoise of caterwauling.
Exchange:

an internment, my interim-marooned
paucity for your best woolen tropes.
Cherub gristle for jock demise.

The cloud machines "much
praise & a little counterpoint,"
down to "Let them eat fur."
(So far *some* "the," eh? That commodity tart.)

Neutering clerk postures gestures "out there," more
choreographers for patriotism by spectacle remove to
spatio-temporal spats. Sit calm, sit tight.
As a talking-to merely descriptions some
recently bought self. "Recently we …,"
behaving-away in a conversational
wish to be taken serially.

Overnight the Banana Republic became the Footlocker.
Where homespun *philos* deletes,
bingo results. (No, but
I believe you were about
to tell me.) Proof of
God the quad or coughing, coffee,
copy.

Strategy rents a hall for the Doubt benefit;
mentions the future as if present fact
in a sit-com destined for re-runs.
I rants on account drawn against for trifling sums.
If we had enough cream then, we went to the lake.
All ways of leaving

the house. The title
was *Hood Ornament*, but
inside was more
beans & rice, rice & beans,
brutal ticks roving initials and a series of baffles.
Saved blocks all occurrences of sought, burbs
on no-good ground, unrealized nest of the frail
hegemony of eyes' constellar bloom.
Reading comfort. Misnomer
of the loner's double-agency.
"Liberal demonology" distances interest,
anticipating impelling presage
hounded by spittle, and a good cry as required.
Devisive links Tex Rabelais to the flinch covenants
of "less illicit, less thrill."

A subject builds in
the shape of subject evasions,
flings shank sweat down the small running fissure,
licks salt against a ripple of identity, yet lacks
the entire in-alley kitchen of the Elsewhere set.

"Notations, though not writing, could be
read by the maker."
                    Lascaux my eye.

The animal, renewed by no muzzle,
yeildeth thyne flowre thinge, coincidence & simultitude,
lofty churlish improbable *recit,*
a low rant dousing
more jargon than actual cash.

            (To wit:
            peruse *this* phatic opulence, Mort.)

Assert has a CERTAIN cachet:
The cute-with-a-vengeance pseudo-Elizabethan argot
genuflecting before the tatters of oracular orifii. Gimme
my sequined glitterati back, my barebacked
ducats too. Lucid
tactic wefts of finale
disaccomplished by *l'Academie,* winging
procedural sideswipes,
clod dross,
ex cathedra pronouncements, mores & more
wide-angled pariahs than you can stick
shakes to period.

If first thought (Sony!) is corporate thought,
the margin is where you *can't* focus on
the benighted beach of "needless to say."

The popular prank imitates
Harv's Business School, meretricious,
microcosm-enhanced, too angry
to consequence, the problem being
both "deeply funny" & "moving" in a book.
"Roman," I said, "you'll just have to
trust me on this one."

All this upscaling of the *usée*, the new
reticent format gambit of *The Compleat Caretaker*,
incremental slips, broken by laughs,
lowjinx & chipdip excitement,
years of baffling neglect grapple,
extrapolate the "boneheaded blunder"
of the subordinate.

She (singer) parts time, he
(open fire) permits of
Contextual Collectables shoppe. Buy it
second-hand, you still have to
break it in. Wan
bungle in the Harlem could mean.
(Only the Strong Sur-etcetera, Ur-
etcetera.)
Tearing lost cat reward
at the edges where

the surplus is weather, its nyms
& norrations. "Be" film, all gory.
I decided to re-read it in the original,
(penumbra, porch, pratfall)
"from its very *inception,*
as it were." As if

the long throw to first were
49 per Kapita pages
of Neighbourhood Watch. Intention
hamstrings proportion (the salesman's
"opening" salvo), portent
caudillos the pseudo-scientific bravura
of New Age entrepreneurs. A "turnout"
is not a "general strike."

Text incapable of quelling the internecine,
mystical sputum, hemorrhages of spiritualization.
"Sanitized" collaborationists quaff
Flag & Tether Ale awaiting the grilled
bream of confirmation.

As a "concession to *divertissement*" the 4 a.m. Medical-Dental
collapse just grazes the witty Viennese polemicist in us all.

A parable is heard off-stage, another
word, another error of omission intersects
a delicacy & a plain-
clothes conversation.

Samizdat something.
Trumped-up curios, maps blank
by going. Patiently
waiting to merely practice
rueful shrapnel brickfest &

thumbnail fish-barrel shot of
disruptive colouration.
Rankle memorandum straddles a catch-all,
die-hard hyphenation. Nothing quite
satisfactory, quotable. Nonetheless,
she *did* get off that chemical
quip at the weapons conference.

Now to hash-out a sequel: Nebbish
Bob, the lonely ocarina salesman, our nabob of dust.
And beloved covert catalyst. Fundamentalist
farm-team convinced the walls would best
in khymer beige. In imported memory.

KATHRYN MACLEOD

The Infatuation

being the most ... considered dangerous
... most women in America ... not yet
... left the city with a gun ...
dark skin, leach ...
button, button up ... keep it hard the whole time
... over something small, sedative ... inner thigh
surprise revulsion, strokes ... peaks interest
about his whole life, sadly
a cold room, leftover ... male eggs
... lounge, elevator shaft
... ambitious interloper ... entering
pleasure with tools ... reduced me
... our event horizons ...

infatuation ... sweet smell, protrudes
room deaden nightly, bisect ...
... bolted, swept clean, leaks ...
... revealed a white face ...
a lot more where that came from, he
has a lot more ... ditch it ...
... take more pictures of me ...
winter in the apartment ... gentle male
companion ... inspired tongue and finger
using things that don't belong to you ...
improve my position ... critical fantasy

disbelieve the education, jealous
… close the room up, cure this …
acceptable sexual combination … our sympathy
… not adequate to be your father …
personal reticence, intellect, breasts …
child's play… titanium …
tell a good one, lay a finger on him, open season
… easy ideas to digest …
… don't push his buttons …
damp shirt … warm smooth bellies, fifty-fifty …
… give in to a good time …

respect the tyrant … a complete withdrawal …
… making you touch me …
isolated study of the male organ …
… exhausted idea, room foreshortened …
teach us, heal us, sleeping … hard
inside my palm … on the way to the top
more money than the others, prudent …
… the mother stopped the father …
weight room, weight of consequence …
… displaced commitment, belted up …
forgive me. I've enraged you.

… messy liquids … uninvited failure
a collection of substantial size …
your nipples visible through t-shirt …
… exchange an old one for a new one …
brief morality … angry about "the masterpiece"
unmaking the bed. evasive.
… completion or celebration, erected
out of boredom … my right point of view …
relax/antagonize … complete the sentence
        … his hard line …

… hesitant. undulant. undefined …
… going forward from the word go … making
this history thing … implying a common background …
future after you answer the question …
… eyes out for: give me real examples …
let me speak outside the family.
… don't need a sisterhood, a real threat …
essential holiness/her complicit soldier …
… you don't need courage with a mother …
we fall short. police protection.

I deliver you …
… correct me if I'm wrong … revealed
by how much you know you own, a style
of employment … heterosexual blossoms colour
… infrequent visitors, to be a maverick
I need you/envy me my freedom …
… my life escapes context …
    … going all the way back …
… black-hearted momma, keep me clean …
family vertigo. trash victims

… redemption/flagellation/torso …
… virile girls for men …
this is great art.
… *I'm on the very bottom. I have*
no way out. I have no one to talk to …
Listening pleasure. Listen to their pleasure.
… you speak filth … relieve yourself …
you speak the truth …

… relieved of her responsibilities …
a model for the neighbourhood …
… sexual arsenal … delicate subversive …
punitive silence, sentenced to naked women …
… dreams of a long cock betrayed him …
the dimpled skyline …
Bus to the hotel. A great city.
I can buy anything here.

Asylum

A fugitive longer than expected
out of the pit, darling
It was good sex, Mary
down on my knees everywhere, everything
touched became hard, longer
than expected under the mound
A monumental longing

I love large birds, it reminds me
how much dirt in my fingers transforms
a level of selflessness
two of us fucking two more of us
the blood stops, here, houses
touch, stucco to thigh
awake after the voices, an eruption

This is the garden he spoke of
rejoice with rich preconceptions
more fingers unburdened extended
the glue fixed, a vacuum
of culture abruptly resolved, down
on my knees almost everywhere, spoke
to the right Power

Seeing it everywhere, everything speechless
and untouched
hold tight to the breast
the breast speaks
the landscape avoids exact repetition
"Come down from the mountain"
July was especially cumbersome, praying

These are common limits
of custom or candour
voices like voices give me direction
Here, on the lawn, I got out of the lawn chair
onto my knees
his hips move in slow circles
the insects the illness
I'd rather have faith in you
than anyone

Clean truth, undistorted
he stopped in the road
implored us to kneel with him
I can't replace my words
with yours, uncomfortable
distance from distance

It was a good answer
repeated, I met his eyes when he spoke
about how bad it had been
Ripeness, the overflow
a passion for floral
my crimes against nature
for the helpless

Rules involve breakage
a cure for palsy, for baldness
I am speaking hysteric
require an audience
another tongue in the wind keeping
an eye on the time
a story, tell me my story

All this, must come to a Jayl
or Bedlam
all I'm meaning
is narrative I answered
my own question
we stopped in the street
they were marching abruptly
where were we marching

A good prayer, a plea
for safety your guilt
as secret as eaten, these hours
are all that I'm worth
the excess an envelope
extremities hands
clasped

My Visions memento
a belief in it is what
I believe I remember
a long line or lost heritage, laughing
the old way under the trees
the park is pleasant and safe

Escapes ruins or ruin
little rice greens a simple
spreading outward, a branch
or our veins, its
exact meanings concentrate
all the past selves
the queue waiting for cash
or to speak to

Arms outward you will not fall
this time, close to the ground
new clothes still wrapped in plastic
the meal hardly touched
a panorama this moment
they're everywhere, floating

One Hour Out of Twenty-four

I · a Country of Ease and Blindness

The fish leapt from the water with rejoicing and were drowned in air

    the streams dried from exhaustion

        the corn burned in the fields.

outside in darkness
watching yellow rooms

the first husband died
the cat moved away with friends

the sun rose and fell a thousand times
winds blew, stinking of tar and chemicals

refugees moved in and were evicted
friends revealed themselves as enemies

great doctrines stumbled
letters were mailed, came back unopened

she returned, and walking up the stairs
she limped

II · Winds Blew

It was a fourteen dollar gift. Enough, I felt, to win me favour.
We took feathers, beads, and herbs, some sort of bird or other

    baubles symbolizing hope.

There is so little of it.
If I had more money and more relatives, my life would be easy.
I gave up the baby, started drinking.
We must have drank a thousand babies into being.

I found more silence than imagined. SHE appeared to me in all
    her glory.
I was embarassed by my longing.
Ill at ease and awestruck.

We imagined pictures of ourselves.
I closed my eyes and saw a waterfall

one's greatest fear, falling

    out of context, three decades

        give me some hope

           we have everything but this

III · Glory

> "I enjoy a picture of myself
> as sturdy, shouldering the weight
> of unrequited love, or braving
> life with all its unforgiving
> unrelenting trials"

Shot in the knee by a Colombian drug lord. Scarred by machetes in African warfare. Abandoned by your parents in an American slum. Baptized in the ocean by a pastor in an undershirt.

> "my faith unbending"

I know Meaning and its trickery. The corpse under the fallen leaves.

IV · Inside out

Still. The air is moist and warm, an old shawl worn with comfort.

The day opens into the old orchard. The house is inside out. I am waiting in the garden for the animals.

Motherhood required more and less in those days. She never would play softball. The smell of dust and heat betrays me. Or backstage, the muffled sound behind the curtains, waiting for the first cue.

The music. The impulse to believe is still the same. The one and only home run.

V · One hour

the romance of the past, bundles of herbs
a spell or curse, the shaman, priestess, ascetic

all this for love, years
were wasted
shamefully, the greatest player
of them all

the rifle cocked, a shot
across the street, an earthquake
illness felling thousands, boys
specific words are not allowed

to speak of human
process, like a clock, computer
syntax, missing children
in the church's care

if I allow myself
to look back, imagine how they live
in fear, ten dollar purchases, the great
depression left them living

one hour out of twenty-four
the first word of courage
SHE is floating in the sky, sad angel
off-key, yards of crinoline, toe shoes

I risk my intention. Life doesn't
catch up with activity
rags of information flutter
love, after all, astounds us

DAN FARRELL

Thimking of You

all there was that
was really spread every way
but it was but for a few
it quickly it every day
but had been set down of
besides others concealed
it for itself
to what followed
set in hot
it for calculating
be seen but
that there was no
those that would this hurry
and the more pass with them
to them to note
the one was the carrying
to be some were low
there was none and of
within in that is to say
in all there was upon found
had still the beginning
there was but
but it was but for a few
and found that
though they though the
they set down

found there but had been set down
may not be of one farther for
perhaps as well than it could be
much in the hands of such
to leave them all as things in such
advising with him
what he had it seems
as that you as to a please where
in a manner all and as many did
because so at last
way other off for that time
away was always cross'd to take in
off again what to do in it
safely take them
they regard one another
to going away
it came very warmly from something in them
it did not evidently point out
stay and take
when and where
midst be made more
indeed to submit
and that then away was to attend
at the same
might either
was a few
and of
of it
as to and who do but to resolve
wholly apart to
to have from

had from
had what
this lay
than ever be kept this that turning
that as was meet
and all had a farther
that if order also
immediately had found out there
being both in
rested put off
now and towards
it didn't come straight on towards
over for tho'
indifferent upon than last
at length where it began
that in this
in the next
no more and while
things soon changed
thickin in
in comparison of that went by ordinarily
went generally
once in or in had givin
and of the last
that any should have
midst of so hardned
not say quite
many ways began now
there were
even all not in such
in such a manner would be really none

now out
            much as touch them
            hardly any thing
      not want being told
            bringing that
        now the particular part
all together or within all look'd deeply
            it possible
        gone into where it pleas'd lessen'd
            every where presented fill them
            must make just might well towards the latter end
      not so much some times to the other end
            the most surprising thing set
            way were went up
            way not mingle were very many
on one have gone the length
        at a loss chiefly before themselves
first frequent
                  whole mass upon the whole early
first in a most often
      meet with smells
        depend upon being over even
drew who depended upon consequence
        in and about number of whom
        this was then
            they were encreas'd
            not so large than as there
      in otherwise that belong'd everything
forgot such their
            settle always a notion to have it above
      grown were assembled together and put back

from the face
but a few so many
there was any before there did
that it that the pass'd directly
was of a feint
that they not only little
it as found in it not rise
that same their
the even of their the that like their less
motions part
been what they will than ever they were before or since
repeated ever find him to stop
that ever last degree
these put abundance
no even out of gone
breach one saw one
going in a time bright on one
side on the left on the right hand more to the right
now to one to
did not see it as so narrow that knew of it
plainly any account intimating
run upon a most
moderate taken up them in was
sunk out of them no doubt did
least in proportion draws rather to turn to drives
calls of all least
fled presented what it tended
not been kept that kept up and undone
impossible and the working away manner to again
but had provided to forget and had not such second
by way

there was often no near
their share had been set up were shut up
sat upon the Contenances
omit remote from
who fed that they ran
Potions themselves before-hand
incredible and corners
exact in case
set off was found out a number
did nothing
had a preparation Confusions fitted after
off with crossings but there beyond all this am
certain written on them
I might lock myself in a Time
thrown into remains
the Hurry the first relate rather to take to be from
when spread soon
not knowing what then their what themselves
from with repeated
reads not relish
hover their faces some
just Alarm
concealed would heard
none of aloud along
Hesitation to be begun to
running into above
done that this down
drove could sober
brought to a next of the most
could good for nothing
but expect should

far as that they nor
prevent a the Errand
by to by lessening and
        restoring could not mention now
what frequent Regulation
            I happened at shutting
follows happy
    same space so if any
every what
            every for every there
lock attend until
            places most Quarter
Severity of if uncertain or it
        be very begin
houses their stirring at
but by but by
            least in order little
shut the volume of the down out from itself
        as I went along did I stay one
    sent him of no heard
    heard at or a last of that was this
no would then
        what to make out The
    long of them went it was to them
            as they thought Bolts on
        next go that help
            miserable up them
    escape would the usage
    side as there by are a back
            found nothing stir to
break yard and back between

depended than
 any forward of those lodge
interval a thing the family
  admit you neither off remember I Nor
   driven that I am either when they were out
  whose near back to the Case
  and shut by
   I think I hear the airing
    which less call it
weekly out of return in after seldom giving got thought it
 Tents by me
    late had abouts shift
    who first where to go set
follow can that Length looked had
all that the middle which brought
  such a by East turns
 but the loose were their threw
  describe about a little cold
  able to those
    run all refuse
  I had not been running
    I could not hear backward
 as near to be
  on the hand we found some narrow cases
 at the stay once first twice
pass this one is what a scarce these these were in hard
  a break had come how spread
one that one that
  the extended under
 cold of that there most that many
    then end then the end heard in

on at least it was opposite
finding calling to the door it
        the numbers had found a mouth
    waited coming down
    at add the article
            mention that take off the money those behind
            went in that two kind of laid enough
            few had broken in to sea
                they could be relieving the watching
    the number was watching every ten
                nine carried the place to dark
                which pit a pit saw under the compass hand
hedge cast the long and
                puts the side within green field leaden
                morning lost the less notice
        lain had it bread to left
        the thousand greater the distracted one naked
during the windows I repeated the doors
                    long from that train had made a leather sum
            in half it brought down to bind
to sleep into it the pool an 8th
                    a tar came to total them
before her arms distracted in a sitting weight
                first the fly had no room for killing
            it came to cases to lay the usual spot
            whole ear cases back parallel themselves
part sleepiness part stirs recording risen in to the lime sides empty clothes
    what it added to the judging more lame more the third man
                load at a safe go last faces at a time
        a narrow bow in the height was hottest at the river he brought
        staying or just by dry got what towards cut

stint cut out of a block back on
no quarter to think old orders to raise for it
divide first ought to
down their sack that their head broke out
pass on to six to send without such as four to look out
if they had were out little they laid
under halted out to having them as they sound
would it already stone
in two names would have the room pay
into who even midling got to and
those had and sides on or by as in as to tilts
usage were that others less
an eye anyone that say thing
for counted but under to not
not or any they degree
face as it persons after it persons this
say cast it is in stop
begin or in really large sequences
less of the end
I would accept in shutting
running up when would continue to hold
both room an employment
came in two to take still
meeting whether to describe
stood me brain as you out
flung had before were shifted
his bitten his on
were ripen to again cold other
had had last
stark to one they were a height of
ware runs cases out of their one

the fire had fallen next to the state
  declare us this office a speaking sake
            out of his deeper dancing row
run than to full them open
laying saw it hot health
            I kept beginning compounded
      the closing seems to influence myself
      better to look scarce than remember the numbers
      the widening hand it
bring us a channel end
            tied to his both
      number going to drive on
         shall false
thousands of case
money was the suppy
            city the provisions
and quit doing their low
      to record those wonderful minutes
      those spots came
         then I am a kind of score
      tenth it
   eggs them as find
one to on one long on to recess frozen longer
draw a tine to had
broken the warm
            Time began but in winds
warm or a horse pass
desire may not be of one
      without that desire he should keep his permission
   manner was end
            spread the pretensions

a face to see as stomach to pocket
next destinating to go
dearest stoutest voice
gone to due
side as it smells
who would Romans
tampering to fill a pawn
you give the stairs your words for nothing
only unperforming those
leaving old comets
tears of deal for further in the barn
the medicine was seized in their mouths
copies like
when the order I am searchers
refusing to that
before the hands shut the bedding her purple
any lecture is the bedding sound are
the love for keepers
dinner put in Monday volume
delude in the house the shift must bulk
knocking on his body he came down on his wringing
now the coming sea water
nothing might be in the house
face without calling
stall near her driven to spread talk
for hand barns thing barns
not her compass but deep dressed
stark had the safety of restraining in posture
little relation's caps drown the sound
thinly instances instead of one pest
might the middle of sound be set to end

laid the leg had no length but a bearer in blankets
speaking pretend to call to condition
body who talk to dead knowledge brewing
swoon went away stood
swellings in time
slight face from where you were wet
thought it sent him through flannel
to his breasts to fit proof
the looking inside of her candle
nearer in words to her nose
sprinkling in or out I am writing this step
breaking them stores
a box is tools for a comical town
quit my pit
knowing to be frightened in
surrounded scent of account bands
fetch lie dead
miserable Eastern
distracted together
quicken and rotted
belonging for a sound
an indication of pan yelling here
seen any side except
bones with long poles to cover
end which the strange sea might blow
a height I expired
low face down mine pointing my smooth setting purse
clock tale of a clout
slipt himself sleep
hats the first to be big
losers of their paper's self

in the piping well-minded pause
our instrument without our spreading vast December water
                    it may dry the following poor years
        compared to a few beans
a little with a little end
        after the powder 'til the shook of hot ears
                stir a grass field
                        steets they could zeal
        sleep by my fasten
            a guess as the hill ruining
                    it had twice as sex
        setting the air red
            grown short shut
                        day stone
            freshest nothing bring the mind just to the stands
and drive to Time again in May
        unmovable woody body
        bowels send to them slowly love
        staves made
                    creature near them and knew
                    open so near shore
        disparity to spot on a word
                    touch lower to the roads
nothing proportion to remember
                        emptying cats must stand it taken
            grows a pattern for recording
        stirs kept number out of five
        added to set lime beating
                in the next wind set
He said he was a small tent and damp
                    fig a time

fields of the passing pieces
raised their hottest
            up certificate of still
ford stand his name
           there but a direction in the band
while the mud kindled
face as a space of error
        I did a little left
    did to sight a drawers
        she thought I laughed but I looked narrow
     sudden came to be sudden nothing
   invitations doubt
      swarm lives in a velvet kind
    a black quack yes
cases hung staring into the impenetrable yards
   s   omit the awake
knees reflections
under the trees out of their shape

Thimking of You was written while reading
Defoe's *A Journal of the Plague Year.*

LISA ROBERTSON

from The Apothecary

Tersely I find myself beginning with the letters *gl* instead of grass undeniably to found a presumption of intimacy and station upon myself which would seem to speak not of that scission but of the really normal beauty still floundering between my teeth just as within the wilder dominion urges entertain and puddle seeming to offer proof that weekends once so drowsily crouched and now algebraically supplied attach tenderness to symmetrical and embroiled vocabularies.

Here the urge is strong to choose confusion and recast my dialogue since I impose a skittish requirement which does not meet my real needs although I speak from the perch of a consonant too distant to be sedulous and I feel like theorizing or sense the emotion of theorization like the built image of a prudent and coppery dime deflected from substantial to accidental manners – I felt so shredded that I bewildered myself with parts and it was inevitable that the recognition would swell into routine but ploddingly revived with fine clothes and a dashing audience I had to tingle thinking how this would be a little early…

I want an ingenious fibre to be treated as funny tragedy expressing a classic argument against materialism which runs like this: which changes of costume are bound to be dangerous? what code is honest and practical yet marginally corporate? which motives may have been under cultivation? how is my courtship skittish? can a fabulous correspondence lapse into notoriety? which source shall I accommodate? could tearing be the worst thought to realize? may I run my hand over the photograph and feel absorbed? would hilarity be thick enough to noticeably bream the hectic pinks and sullen purples? again I ask, what is throttled?

I depend on the botanics of abuse pistillate rather than floundering but still link guilt to a hectic perennial that coaxes me to reject the swaying cradler though shot silkiness of the neighbourhood seemingly parses or sheathes my lacquered act or flounders in a scission so isolate analytic ardent yet drowsy that I need only repress the metallic expression of the diary with some gliding veil of dust.

The seemingly lackadaisical newer and wonderful fake melds a thought held nicely as an idea of confession or cumulative stain even critically apathetic regenerating the notion of misunderstanding as an essay – what of the loose strength of the other side of the structure tending to roll like a violated paintbox – but my digression has not questioned the interior of the computer where familial semblance in the computer of broken branches brazen angry or skeletal coaxes different kinds into lineups otherwise said bled idiot and rind keening or blister the gender of the clothing remembering how as a boy I felt wainscotted by an aspect of familiarity as if nervous phrases thought beneath expression went parallel to mealtime.

Because I am curious I was giving it to myself in the parking lot but as an absent cause it is inaccessible like the guilt of a double or that *subject* percolating through the illusion of the broken window until peeled and stuck an enigma becomes impoverished by my secret method or my pregnancy my television my jam-jar my animal the stolid waver of my hands my secret method my television – the nervous possibility I deserve.

To generate and stimulate *my Cause* a jar shrunk to an ikon offering a peephole out of the joke where in great respect I shred my traditions and become opaque or contoured in a coppery net, miffed like the thigh of a gender tingled in a category with no concern for the future, scraped by an old anklet – volatile crusted absent to witnesses – unless having carefully studied the essential part of the stained presentation my action trembles as though some causal chain has been defined as the shimmying throat of an alphabet.

from XEclogue

How Pastoral: A Prologue

I needed a genre for the times that I go phantom. I needed a genre to rampage Liberty, haunt the foul freedom of silence. I needed to pry loose Liberty from an impacted marriage with the soil. I needed a genre to gloss my ancestress' complicity with a socially expedient code; to invade my own illusions of historical innocence. The proud trees, the proud rocks, the proud sky, the proud fields, the proud poor have been held before my glazed face for centuries. I believed they were reflections. The trees leaned masochistically into my absence of satisfaction. The horizon pulled me close. It was trying to fulfil a space I thought of as my body. Through the bosco a fleecy blackness revealed the nation as its vapid twin. Yet nostalgia can locate those structured faults our embraces also seek. A surface parts. The nasty hours brim with the refinements of felicity. It's obvious now: Liberty has been dressed in the guise of an ambivalent expenditure.

My ancestress would not wait for me. I began to track her among the elegant tissue of echoes, quotations, shadows on the deepening green. Because she bore no verifiable identity, I decided to construct her from kisses: puckers and fissures in use, and also from the flaking traces of her brittle skirt. For I needed someone not useful to me, but obnoxious, prosthetic, and irrelevant as my gender. Let's say Nature, like femininity, is obsolete. She's simply a phantom who indolently twists the melancholic mirror of sex. Far into the rural distance, the horizon splays beneath her florid grip. In deep sleep, my ancestress tells me a story:

"Ontology is the luxury of the landed. Let's pretend you 'had' a land. Then you 'lost' it. Now fondly describe it. That is pastoral. Consider your homeland, like all utopias, obsolete. Your pining rhetoric points to obsolescence. The garden gate shuts firmly. Yet Liberty must remain throned in her posh gazebo. What can the poor Lady do? Beauty, Pride, Envy, the Bounteous Land, the Romance of Citizenship: these mawkish paradigms flesh out the nation, fard its empty gaze. What if, for your new suit, you chose to parade obsolescence? Make a parallel nation, an anagram of the Land. Annex Liberty, absorb her, and recode her: infuse her with your nasty optics. The anagram will surpass and delete the first world, yet, in all its elements, remain identical. Who can afford sincerity? It's an expensive monocle."

When I awake I find myself in a new world. The buildings, the clothes, the trees are no more or less coy than they were, yet I had been so intent on the dense, lush words that I had not realized a world could be subtracted from her fruiting skin. The old locutions could only lose themselves in that longed-for landscape; but now I pluck for myself "peace in our own time" and the desuetude of nostalgia. It's as if suddenly a pitcher of slim flowers needled that monumental absence of regret. So elegant, so precise, so evil, all the pleasures have become my own.

Eclogue One: Honour

I have felt regret but turn now to the immensity of a rhythm that in the midst of her own mettle was invisible. I'll describe the latinate happiness that appears to me as small tufted syllables in the half-light, greenish and quivering as grasses. Ah, the tidy press of the catalogue, the knotted plantlets of a foiled age, the looming test of our grim diaphany, let me embrace these as the lost term "honour" while I lace this high pink boot I call Felicity.

(Lady M finds her thoughts a little agitated; her sight wanders and is fed by an artificial rudeness whose particular odour floods her mind. It's as if she were dreaming on a bus.)

Watered patterns sway lit beneath the air or beneath the movement of air. Fine grey pigments cling so pungently with such rich spread that it's all dainty and silken as the fickle-stench of the sibilant and caressed name "Nancy." The teenaged multitude drifts off to a grainy and torpid horizon; they stroke the crude till it compels or decadently blooms. Banality stokes their punctual lust for the familiar; branches, courage, obligation stalk as cathartic yellow splays among roots. Weeds often seem sardonic as the measured tactics of a cold strut; yet if leisure were conquered this landscape would gauntly bud and split into the cold texture embroidered on the lurid skin of a leaf.

Or: careful field quincuncial as the exhaustive and private happiness spilt from a necklace of januaries. Knots, compartments and grottos cannot compare to a field's livid frisk, neither to the ridgie factions near the pompous arch. Yet the sky's tolerably liberal and apt to supplement a bitchy little tapestry, in the way the light in a painting seems fringed or redolent as a pimp, in the way a teenager will flagrantly caress a name with paint. Read this orchard as the Roaring Boys who course the town at night: tawdry, flecked and billowing behind their silky fluted pricks, their short lines syncopate as ripe fruits shake the lawn.

Or: she's in the landscape without ambiguity and it's to a trim cloister she lends her tendentious support. Wind preens or lustres the elegant weeds; obligation splices cold and keeps darkening and brooding. The weedy ruffling of Nancy's sheathed hips absorbs a thought quicker than the lagging wind. Everything patterns a differing lag – the flanked and massy sky turns decorative as it clusters or nearly punctuates her torpor. The Roaring Boys fan back; they coil poignantly beneath the moral clusters of their blue groves. The roaring angels are alert as nets and their sly pricks nudge the cold.

LADY M   *I feel hapless when I think of the buttery and peculiar*
flowers we dub the monikers of our malaise.

NANCY   *Yet it's so plucky and slightly ruffled …*

LADY M   *As this dim foliage we stride through. Nancy, what of "par-*
adise" or "harmony"? It's so leather-like in unreality –

NANCY   *We're professionals. I see your face in the rain.*

LADY M   *Like a grim violet.*

NANCY   *I push you away*

I fall to the floor

It's a mixed-up world

With shook-up love.

LADY M   *My back's to the wall. How can such slim felicity so bruise*
the trees?

NANCY   *You call this filial conduct? Stop there. I hear the Boys:*

ROARING BOYS   *Hey Blushing Berries, you've got us curious. Groves*
(singing)   *Nodding can't masque your emotion's curious*
Fretwork. We need consolement. We're no strangers
To the quick whirls of russet-wrapt or bluish
Emotion, pendant, typical, sultry, fringed
Like a bump on the horizon. Our reddened silks
Rustle with profession. Imitation cramps
Such rudeness: But those games just aren't interesting.
Take this hint – we're typical Boys, our fickle emotion
Wanders and is fed, yet we choose
To dedicate our follies to you. Shall we syncopate
The several beauties known by the name of the Purling
Stream? This tumult's meant to tilt
All grammar. We're just those that
Want you to feel…

Dear Nancy,

Quietly, evil as a concept's disappeared and I'm not sorry to judge the
smoothed-over garden dangerous. I've indulged my curiosity in all
the horrid graces, thought swelling or swollen, conscious anyway
that the motive seemed creepy – but it seemed natural. Their diction's
pleasure unwound me, though I knew it doggerel, and they mere
poetasters. They've not advanced from the flimsy past: it's just the
tumult of a pendant usage, it's just the sultry horror of that fake for-
est. Choric swains that call me Berry miss the point – dirty little
swains playing at the mouth of the gemmy cave, fraying my nerves
with their meticulous blossoms. So I'll loosen up to describe their
limbs as botanical manifestations of small irksome enjambments,
styleless as numbered doors. Yet silk and cotton and solid some bird
or some robin flew through the somewhat florid expansion once
named as my heart. It was noonish and the pinch held out to a per-
son anyone would name trouble…a girl whose instinct for trend was
marginalized and pointless. But I wanted something new, something
way past the florid radicalism of the Marxist cashbar. I wanted the
stuff that joyriders run on: that queer touched-up light that transmits
over the air; miming a tension, living on the crux of a regime which
could slide to the coy illusion of Liberty.
    Typical girls – whose liberty leaches and fans from a porous bor-
der, who fold like fans, who trick the eating class – typical girls
explain to me the use of the word "Liberty." I'd fall to the floor for
their smooth gesture, their opaque and viscous oil-like drag, their
porous border, their controlled iridescence, their drag and tooth, the
gnarled yet polished scent of evil. When I'm trying to think about the
word "russet" I use fan-like tactics borrowed from the girls, though
vagueness signals, almost breaks my purple spite. It's not easy to

define my feeling of a reddened peace of mind, a ruffled, shattered, mixed-up world. How can silence or expression stop? All these sluttish thickets and rivulets of green, all these bitchy, sybaritic flickers of leaf only simulate my technical and carminine thirst for the smooth sensation of felicity. A spilt necklace makes a curious fretwork; yet I've indulged my curiosity within a knot, judging the drag and density viscous and gaunt. Maybe it wasn't the girl, maybe the Boys took a smile from their package – it was raining, they weren't looking at me – maybe they've wreathed their instinct for thought.

There's no need for crying. Honour nor emotion's not so squalid and swindled as all that, though I feel the grim vibrations of the darkening air, I feel the horrid crackling transmit through my skin and hair. It's so reptilian like those weird things that scuttle underfoot, lend their frenzied rhythm to my thought

> those peculiar monikers
> those russet quivering stalks
> those lags
> those plantlets
> those elegant and massy coils
> Nancy, how can these be *Thought?*

– Lady M

COLIN SMITH

Straw Man

Sits beneath immaculate drone of rows of square fluorescent suns.
He works day in day in talks serial bits
to colleagues whom no one knows. Herringbone
staples. Would someone please tell him the colour of this
year's power tie or if such icons have meaning
any more red handkerchief in right
hand back pocket why not vote for tyrants who lay claim
to resurrection of economies. Armpit fetish.

Pregnant is an entire department of data processors.
Lately there's a water cooler to worry about sometimes
goldfish with empty knowing eyes
appear inside, he knows that water conducts sound
(and thought?) better than air.

Dear Valued Customer,
keeps his nose pressed to attention
play out play out. He keeps a bottle of Glenlivet
in a drawer marked "Materiel." Selfhood under "Explosives."

Senses stanched with cotton.

. . • . .

I am Buster Keaton with neuralgia, Henry
Spencer with a poisonous erection.

Caught buying food, and the same seismic embarrassment
as if caught buying pornography. You confuse
your singleness with your aloneness. You can't be saved
– just recycled. You could be seen
as Calvinism's failure or future. He felt

like a struggling starlet. Not that
starlets struggled, they merely lay back, opened their legs,
and welcomed America. Tempted to stick out
his ego, thinks every ambulance must be for him …

.   .   •   .   .

At home he makes an ornament sandwich, perambulates
while chewing, you *would* live in a cube. Not much
to see out the window. Phlegmatic weather, a landscape
real but exiled. Networking
nirvana. Robbery modem. Peking man on a menu. Restaurants
    fewer
can afford, bulletproofed. Though the poor are tough and stringy.

More cautious to stay inside and tend to ferns. He lards
pepper at their bases, protection from the cat. Indoor jungle,
light wood furniture, skyscraper bookshelves, reasonable art
on white walls. One kit one bat one bed. He rereads
history and works at drawing connections. Swills philosophy,
waiting on that one line someone may have written

that might help him. Turnips at dinner, he is how much light fog.
Often unsure of having a soul so much
as a batch of cultural inscription.

Library take-out, pretence cure. I read
aloud, Wittgenstein for the cat Elmore Leonard for myself.

After dark all the plants breathe in. "I can't be bored
– I'm watching TV." Goes to sleep
with cucumber slices fixed all over his face.

· · • · ·

Dear Memo, Dear _____:
Your gratifications and punishments are a streamlined dud.

Juniper
hangover, singing
Twiddish in the shower. Car alarm
wails "I have something to lose
I am made of more than you."

I am not *chosen*
but have applied for the job.
I've always wanted to be a Government
of Canada initiative. Starves his body down
so his erection will be proportionately larger.

Good listener as lethal weapon.

·   ·   ●   ·   ·

(Solicitous on a living-room wall a shrinkwrap
of *New York Movie* by Hopper. Obsessive as vitamins or sales
tax, he fixes on this image, lets constitution go in high wind
pointed into the palace's excremental murk, at icy fragment
of screen where two adipocere lovers negotiate some affection.

Travails travels trawls ghostly these glum fixtures, down
stairs, up red stripe of navy-blue uniform of beautiful usher alone,
blonde long hair pale face somehow pinched and soggy, black hole
of a flashlight curled into her palm, is he here – her?
is he dim rich hat gold cord black shoe gold button white cuff
        locked
thought red miniature lamp may be the marbled squirm on the
        carpet

down to accretion spin-dry till Zen and Love redux sprung
heart hotpot accords dead in the bathtub water pillow
rusted out from crying 1939 for her 1985 for him war
dread embedded in nerves calm common

denominators for them both.)

·   ·   ●   ·   ·

You are now beginning this month's menstruation.

His orgasm more of an epileptic seizure.

Sacred = scared.

After what was or may not have been
the requisite number of sunsets, I was killed
by one male or female item in a red sports car
who had one hand on its career the other on a cellular phone.

But I wish to join the comfort class in the largesse way.

Living in or as a furnished model.

Third day of unwashed genitals deludes him
that he smells like an aroused woman.

Insufficient tits, and the thighs are *all wrong.*

You are trapped in style
habitual.

He is too fond of the word "silence."

I want to open up
a steakhouse called Hormone Shot.

To sweat the bed, to gag in grace.

You have fictional personality based on true stories.

Government town as theme park.

If they fail
to understand
that we bring them
mathematically
infallible happiness,
it will be our duty
to compel them
to be happy.

            . . ● . .

File tab reading _____. Born in a breadbox.
We soaked him. This hero to the quiet life, viscousness
in the kitchen, in a rage witnessed by no one.

He grew tall lacking memory in a medium city
that processes cars for a living. His hobbies as a youth
were applying Push stickers to Pull doors, and hiding
bags of rotten produce in shopping malls. The family
is crystal false as the sitcom cyborgs seen on TV.
Ruins himself reading, vacuous correspondent, is that you
on *Cheers* drinking ersatz hootch? Shrug guilt to deploy
loss before it turns mean. Once per fit he takes
a coarse and trembling grief to sexfilms and then.

His alderman is a vehicular disappointment. On t-shirts,
"Nobody knows I'm gay," "Nobody cares
I'm straight." His favourite album
could be called *Music for Autistics*. Lame wolf lone
Spam wild Smurf duck noir. Once we all bought
a Madonna record and he porked a heated orange
to the bass lines. Paregoric in beef stew?

We know his self-sufficiency and political isolation. He trots out
to vote every few years, but unfortunate governments get in
       each time.
Verdict is intelligent though inattentive? Sweat does not
smell like chicken soup. Home is rent, fleas, a cologne
named Rhetoric rubbed along the inner thighs.

We believe our surveillance is unnoticed.
His private speech turned public
does not. His florid dreams and smallest purchases
are documented in the fashion you expect.

"The fatal results, after sports ..."

                    .   .   ●   .   .

I got so self-righteously angry I thought
my head would host an event
of prompt criticality!

That movie was worth $2.75 of the $7.50.

Just another overprecise pervert?
Barricade your children!
Rub itching powder into all the furniture.

He lives in Fort Polio.

Upon activating the water tap and ceiling fan, you
automatically urinate and defecate.

Your Q clearance glorifies homicide.

Our economy
is one way
of inflicting pain
and no marks.

I use a golden blowgun because I want to wound them
in a deluxe way.

Variations only
of villain, you are not worth even one bistro meal.

You are this
undesignated
disposal site.

Padded elbows or room.

·   ·   •   ·   ·

No call to worry such items now. We are standing
on a vacant blue plain that stretches toward
horizon lines better felt than seen. Hard glaze and
monogrammed suspense underfoot. He digs
for earwax with a toothpick, thinks: cat

fud   365 blue mondays a year?   paradise
braille   white cloak   small change   pocket
pool   ink rolled onto fingertips   blackbirds?   a golem
eats lunch in that park   wherever undercuts   backbeat
more no backbeat   fever?   passport   headed

for the lip of closure? Hopes this is true.
Hopes to be some use.
Having read somewhere
one man can make a difference …

                    ·   ·   •   ·   ·

Jesus wants me for a zombie!

Why are you?

"Fuck you" is no insult stacked against "Sign here."

And we thought you could have
an unmediated miscellany of emotions, did he?

In summer he wanders
about the city in white dirty cotton jeans
ripped asterisk-style in the seat
to provide ventilation and enhance social availability.

Help.

Mate.

The cat's name might be Norman, Wrath of God.

I you them us we, as verbs.

This narrative won't endure. Certainly its provisional
author can't. But a reader could go on forever, and
a womb could go *here*.

Militant Tongue

Once upon ideology, It

(blames a weakening family structure
on pornography, abortion, teen sex, extended bar-room hours
    and Sunday shopping)
conditional pronoun verbs directional articles location, i.e.
I walk across the street. "The Marquise went out at five."
I went inside. Just as my body politic, wrists taped

shot in mouth, wrapped in burlap locked in a trunk
came whanging downstairs from balustrade to newel post
whose euphonies sounded like someone orating the syllables of a
    law
firm name. Hey bitch
why don't you suck the sweat out of my hockey jersey? As per
    Agreement
they get our natural resources we get their labour-camp jobettes,
    intellectual
rather than sensual arousal is what the charter was intended to
    protect, ideas

shoved into a pigeon, have your bagman call my bagman, hey
    bitch
why don't you support our policies in El Salvador? "It'll *really* put
    hair
on your realpolitik!" Add water
on the brain to instant opinion, we are very proud of our working
    class
weapons fodder. She says

"I want a man who'll respect me after I come on his face.

"Maybe everyone's membership to the No

"Bullshit Club expired. Our basic gunk is small bare rooms
in a nunnery found in a slice of cork, the historical outlook
glides into Korsakov's syndrome. The dollar
'signs' all the time, war is presented as surgery, our minds
don't have a mind of their own, Iraqi no-fly zones

"are fruit of the poisoned tree, Jeffrey Dahmer
shows more mock contrition than the President ever will, we'd
        better
kill it before we understand it. Your 'bitch' is code for 'cunt'
for those too demure to be uncivil. You want to believe
my pussy has teeth, I'll let you …"

You wanna step out back for some liberal education!?
You are surplus production. Your "self" is the sales receipt.
So laugh, shitbird, she is large

>   IN THE BASE OF THE BRAIN, AND
>   SWELLS OUT OVER THE EARS, WHERE
>   DESTRUCTIVENESS AND SECRETIVENESS
>   ARE LOCATED BY PHRENOLOGISTS,
>   WHILE THE WHOLE REGION OF
>   INTELLECT, IDEALITY AND MORAL
>   SENTIMENT IS SMALL (we enjoy our curricula

of Great Books because none of them were written by women.
I don't see why we need to stand by and watch a country go
        communist
due to the irresponsibility of its own people …)

She responds, "Lap dissolves
can make us believe anything, as if assuming
such an entity as *ex*-CIA agent.
I brake for transvestites and speed for CSIS, ears out
for the screams of those who can't. The difference between

"straight men and gay men

"is about 4 beers."

> ... with Text and Village Singing
> we pair-bond
> then taper off, America
> Lasters, one free capsule of AZT
> in every dime bag of heroin, the status quo
> is *also* a special-interest group, sly
> and goofy euphemism
>
> we call our orgasms "coming"
> as if en route
> to meet our closest friend
> three long blocks away: nerves
> yammer throughout
> flesh, blood flush
> empathy hookup
> now one block
> working the body
> until technique
> shatters, beauty will be
> compulsive, "HiThere!" and recap
> our day's business so
> I humbly submit
> the word "arriving"
> on some fond grounds
> of playful accuracy ...

Trend over time
lays us in cardboard at Pigeon Park
and eating yuppie landfill, my career option
would be murdering heads of state, to ventilate
is not anarchy, we donate our Miniguns to the squats and
remove the inhibitor cards first as a point of courtesy.
Are you now, or have you ever, clock of the walk.

Are travel books "vacations" for our poor?
You've got a Parliament we've got a Mob you're going
to close all the post offices anyway, the least you could do

is make them concentration camps for the homeless.

To trust only those who brush their teeth with their fingers.

      Imagine every human face
      as a bicycle seat!
      Have you a "smelly mohawk"?
      Do you shave or pluck
      your penis? We don't
      need any "professional images." We live
      between channels on our TV set.

We'll chow down with the good guys
'cause they're less sexist and racist than
those other good guys.

    IS IT POSSIBLE
    TO BE LESS DIDACTIC
    OR MORE RADICAL
    THAN REALITY'S
    GUMPTIONS OF MIRROR?

Most children, having parents, are political prisoners.
Heterosexuality isn't a victimless crime.
Most women, actually or structurally, are incest survivors.
All money is counterfeit.
You can't relax under infostatement.

> A final
> utopia final to write
> a children's book
> called *Spot*
> *the Rot* …

He shifts oleaginously toward his girlfriend and whispers
a boiling-kettle-shaped jest of cigarette steam that says
"I want to *bear your child.*"

Take vitamins in alphabetical order, take off
your press-on genitals. Don't fall in love
with the body double, slamdunk every spin doctor, lay off
the military – make them kill themselves. Heed
what the clitoris says.

We are coming but have not arrived.

Anti Tumblehome
– For our Fallen Comrades

These bloody days, this godawful palace. Tangling the illegitimated suprajective 'wrongside' of the sheets. He often seeks a gentle point to sit through a film – HOW to get into synthesizer position. Quiet edge of attention paid and paid.

This subject to erosure. Not address itself simply. The Wars of the Roses, the mechanical muses of EVERY charted century: these dry, terraced grounds.

In a sense a broad cross of mealy bug & armadillo. Radiator us heat exactly like a dump that foreclosed that irretrievable altogether he pokes around.

Since the great War many battles past Our Big Life & WHY there is no smut in the works. Is his voice furried by sadness? There is a drag none prettier than I produce a direction.

An putative author interrogates her silence. This here ban of intention. So is that a penis in your pocket or you just going to shoot me? I got your goat & I'm burying it. You won't see inertia for dust. THIS then is my beloved, seeking the discretion of the grave.

What WON'T we do for history. I didn't make the team Dad.

& me & the boss talk about Durrutti, listen for posterity, we laugh. Such stamina could fit an easy-going scab beer into the picture. This parochial blur an unfigured smear of ill-met resolution.

I have gum & I know how to chew it. A sampling of the industrial organ. Here we encounter tenor.

As the field mouse regrets her last hole – what will we not hurtle upon our father's plain?

But building this dwelling you thought
only of ramparts and defence:
it is to increase dominion
and power for you;
this towering citadel has arisen only
to excite more restless storms in you.

Fricka. Scene 2, *Das Rheingold*

Midsummer's Eve full moon renders us feckless impunity, such a bargain. Something big is on the waters as I am asleep upstairs. At last it is sad to think of Spandau, of previously unreleased monsters on CD.

Collective (more or less impertinence buggering up flow charts & an CONSTANT prolix perifery meting fringe interference considered to 'Venn' monologues.

Losses are fiercer than merely noting ambiguities inherent could suffice. Butter your guns FIRST – each drop in the bucket smoothes the papers.

It is isolation reduces us to a graveled aggregate of overseen lesions.

Oral Tragedy

Ordinance 'distanced' thus, called 'desire' – 'I' pass out eventually. Often this caught too once smothered discord.

Your hand's nerves cut automotivation catching each OWN clasp all plunder all stud & stake position.

Can he finalize such fragments in said factitious bootybags ? Well, recovery and redistribution may not comply with proprietary dictates. OK. MORE property called pleasure.

It ever looks different if rain say hydro cuts or lightning graphs out strikes so hands dial but like that. A final voice in an ear like a promise.

Post is delivered at all hours even weekends & vanity anticipates though diurnally nonplussed or trust this recurrence.

SENTENCED – the guy who got stuck in a helicopter & a guy that got stuck in the house. All hunkering while down with glanders he WILL order others. Shiftless foci wont observe an onus & left to OWN loss, drawl & stick up our chins. Do make distinct then but where's the difference?

You are left with what you get and
Your love is dross
Well you remain whose world is none of mine
I who lov'st well remain left.

& shall interference come between me? Jar down mine own gritty polish & wonder when saliva segues patina. You get what you are left. While distinctions make pleasures own device or fucking doesn't – hitched to mine caboose maraud or don't.

Appears far greater than all machinery yet always misses affecting more than a few months or paragraphs. Not usually called tragedy, so never looked well as heard disquieting items known better. As bereft of physical conditions.

Still webby seeking ALPO to project costs grants & articulated ranges. Never will a necessary, say, & will not be damned. If pressed it will fold in on itself & look passive as accordianing your needs hope allow. Astride the wringer by the by.

Extinguished, like, and a predilection for abasement sidewinders just off the kitchen & enters to cheers and jowels his may hinder.

This tackle bought an afterthought presented as absence of mind as put out the cat twice and for all I know may be too early now remains with coats at a party. & what AFTER predicted drift part?

Cold moves wierd gusts pushing from the underground & so sounding for all that you say as to the contrary the bus has appeared almost before it is almost no longer worth taking. Am I to tactically avoid this or pen too fine a nib on it?

Descend to a lower conveyance, a few things to watch or something.

This first: I've lived on a lake & not seen it but the happy competence of the postal clerk has prevented my letter to you being delivered to me Monday & my nickname no longer means 'physician', pl. Yet not exactly happy. (Please find enclosed my dumb joke) It has been so very cloudy since my arrival that I haven't once seen the mountains.

PC bagman today pipe unveiling Commodore Omega & surely NOW I have come to CANADA. Democratic.

Even yet I wander into shops seeking clerical intervention – is this uh … SOUTH, bitte? But it is not so much any thing and next time drops be sure to. MATTER really never will.

First: appeared unlike any other – unbidden from out th'mist and all to convey a sense of 'to my home'. There is a big belt to walk & I am MOVED. My position separates & I miss you so. Appearance will deceive & look after.

Unravelling still. Not usually called 'pullman' & also a spike not UNlike the Glass Onion on the Alexanderplatz.

I scratch your back and you regard mine with undue fondness & these too shall crispen dear.

Too down the tube not garrulous & no tweeking conductors some few hummers me too. Too broke to impress myself, the turnstile too intimate by HALF & not ethic either but LACK. Felling between frames its name is yet another thing yet HERE this is nonsense. The wind is painful sulfurous lake not condition but flaw. Show in words of your OWN that which is too early or dissimulate & so foreshortened it's squished. Some more changed & not remorse any less than thought the

streets are not the
colour the sky &
indeferent to place any

more. Just take too long enough do tell to cantered once & better but talk much less guess this thing thingy month long deed or jobbing the work right out of him.

missed the geese massed ashore
greased   afloor
          work no worth
              York

OK. So? Gratuitous OR left nothing but we tell that before and before.

Bordering on this to narrow some rail planner's point is the PCB repository. And the water a battery of difficulties. Electing to distrust place renders unto this a civic wad unconscious even by exaggeration. Remember us who live here and there & even later say they pay no bother to this or that. Wi' its ain desires to scan the trades for quotes & subsidized prospects. So I do worse than shut up. I remain to be seen.

Left to me own device, I fail to inter memory or inter-face dick. Most recently called 'indigence'.

So remit to becalm swells bilging out & about & not worse really than common holdings or so-called indulgence, i.e. 'There are PLENTY'. Matter really never will WHAT?

The dolphins surrounde his owne canoe. ie. some fins not others will not take your life alone. Litter spittle stubs bitter little grabby bugs. They stay where they are. Well met beforegotten. Their eyes he said are like plums & well thus coloured - no less afraid than had no quarter been given & now I use them as work needs to work. As legs get tucked within thick spun lint knits & dubbin must, like salt prevention, be taught us. He will put in the room under back sleeping bags.

Later a long line relax took hold & her legs detucked withunder – disarranged a too too configuration's eyes undampened long enough. She requires too much from that.

From the personal pronouns depend suspensions overlooking gaps nodding into collapse.

A spite witheld Poor Old Lucky – drew either a bead or blank lines neither conceived or formatted. Also known as vitreous floaters. i.e. god'd eyes. Pigeon holes. As when 'mongst the crowds, we ate taters then cake, Poms and Westies – we among them in their midst.

In the foreground is one of those lightbulb stoves that needs too much juice & in the clearing is a bath tub & no good at keeping fire going underneath, just no damn good at all.

Light in shift's emphasis to indicate return or returns indicate place. Necessary focus impossible to all constant drain softening the prints.

NO line to process a need initiates a laugh – as falsehoods are by half good on an empty stomach. Back to twitching all postures part. Also known as nerve damage. i.e. so sad you work on the job.

Forget it forget it & write about US. Despot a viscous mesh apparent; these walls return a favour – ie. bum. Bum, I will meet him in 45 minutes my will disintegrate amen. Taken short shrift so change the lesser nouns, mewling – "Some job" i.e. weasel thrust apparent to talk around your ears "the world". Totems of thought. The gorge.

U Bahn reads unlike kitchen she said suddenly to justify somehow a typical rash about the mouth. Do friends usually not as our decision delight?

Apply those BLOODY goats & elect weapons & THIS incises choice. NOW wintering in The Land of Gaudy Tweeds not ONLY sapped but tuckered, mordant yet twice shy. CLEPT though fairly shunted & EVER abreast of the shore. I am – refascinated by: web footed doggies, distant Alcool in the grog, the possible Mounties worse when constituted by state.

& no thought sovereign & too often dipped though still pretty curtsied in my crenellation. (creaky ingenuity) not usually called 'potassium'.

Get thee outa the ball park, onto the marsh – freeze over morass! Hell yes we will talk. World enough & unbearable though detextable. Picky picky.

Trash resistant crack repellant drone infectant broom retardant ('s disjunct as my rod and my staff – they contort &c. Yea though it wiggles ambitiously nary a fear nor a peep.

Then last week he relegated his wit's end to a grubby 5th in the cellar. Not interesting & missing Don to get it. Pop flies sadder. Not too bad sneakers still OK, forgiven, sleeping on the floor but a desk. It won't ever hurt much & LOOKS bigger in 2D. Each According to needs means more than you got. Really missed later.

Every stasis culls loopy strategies – toothy buggers! Porcelain – so watch it! Lighten up throat crack. More appropriate 'you', for instance: cataloquial shifties less problematic in the 2nd remove.

More pointed as to shear fault than lunge else there's merely outside like – working in on an empty stomach as – collywobbles! you quit your bellyachin. Proportionate 'thou'.

Uh, like them in battle fatigues – paler, more like pumpkins squished into tins ritualized unto another date. There so not ever passion as tactic as filmic sentience as cynic's catspaw as drone foil as tailor's chalk as what one gets as one another as one GET's through as municipal negligence as normal kid rash as an unidentified dominant life form as YOU as in sticking the ivories – that is: most gone suckered, deboned and unbidden.

Once 'imagined' deference, veto I yet unsung – expect this, more angry. Push passion from touchiness (distant from MY liver), more likely called humour…yet I as distinct from tracers as before time rang AGAIN & singly tied the line to sadly crow each benefit away.

So. This's affect as tolerance again it is. She's seen deliberately as distanced from your worst.

Affect demagogue despite blander states to stay it elect.

"They are gone & don't ask so many questions they think you are a dummy".

To gums are inclined to off & begone foreclose to the child's own needs – so, it is certainly not his fault he is called Jason & there her are, trying to be his own person, hurling themselves against the chainlink as a parent arrives early to haul off their little monad.

Rational, like quips of hyper-vigilantes circling infield overlays, WHY?

Oh Hedley elm block please

he's pasturing his rat's disease & even it shopsteward it skewer than holy oak.

About taxi Krakow to demin conspicuously around consuming union suited Mississauga scale lacking that provided trust squished beside punctuation entirely. Bowels to conveyance, defated pinkily. Thus I conquer elves. Wrench quarter camera clock how flat they run.

Thought. Before though MINDING meant loss of sequence.

Fate in abeyance – do pardon my interruptance *slips* like 15 years away from hockey to letters sent to sects of divergence. It depends less from sustenance than provenance, I take it. As NOT what this becomes, not WONDER…ahistorical senses distort drag pass amplify & drug all discursive tension – dominance traces memory's tracks.

A drop in the bucket i.e. Plash.

The wretch he sustained while the little bugger in the East Bloc.

White 4 year old attains class satori via Stephen Foster ballad – 'don't worry lady! I'll get those oppressors! More pass saddened by the ride.

Contrast: caught ever may not *et al* as distinct from murder from pleasure.

Now fixed behindsight rupture off in no time withstanding disclaimer'd rail junctures burgled & YET persist unsalvaged compressed or mounted. Desultory notice whether privelege or riders maintain hereditary link in end rhyme takes stock return.

Caught up in sad tales wise up in due time shut up utterly. Poor fingers now welded of frost yet 11th hour paroles Brainiac's grainy tragion, note orbs. Utterance STUFFED in an history of tissue adhesions.

My gaze is numbered, my days remaindered. Tell you later.

The Worst

If this were merely an eidetic image why did she want to be nursed?
                                    – Carla Harryman, PROPERTY

Nor is this all.

It takes a lot to make me laugh. (LIE)

This: a flaw it is that I talk like: This

Philosophy demands frugality, not torture. (SENECA)

To what, in her opinion, would it be reasonable to commit herself?

As Whomism sticks in the craw, so goes out with your REAL pals.

Abelard's only hope was in the fact that these sentiments were not all from the same source nor of the same quality. Margaritas ante porcos. And she bitterly recalls that she (There are so many who hold views like these) bound herself to this rule without realizing to what she (that the dawn of liberation is a long way off). Was committing herself. Risk glamour 'til tendancy dissipates destruction. Sometimes the very movements of my body show forth the thoughts of my soul, betraying themselves in involuntary words. Do you realize

What I *think* is so obvious does not enter into it. This, however, was not the least of Heloise's objections.

Unlike a flawless tragedy, the elegance of which structure is lost upon those suffering in it, the perfect geometry of 'Dotti Trujillo' was only invisible from the air.

There is no mistaking these accents, and, as we shall see, Abelard has taken care not to reply ironically on this point.

If I lived alone, alone I could type through the night. My word broke. (She is describing with heart-rending simplicity the most tragic of all conceivable situations).

Cannot stand on its own.

4 years back) in a (specified); (but by whom) neighbourhood.

                                                        Long way off.

Her submission, accordingly, is not part of recorded history. I am still young and full of life; I love you more than ever and suffer bitterly from living a life for which I have no vocation. Why did they name you?

From then on, Heloise and Abelard saw each other but rarely and secretly, taking every precaution not to reveal their marriage.

She could not bear to make me suffer. In point of fact, any cognitive thought whatever, even one in my consciousness, in my psyche, comes into existence, as we have said, with an orientation toward an ideological system of knowledge where that thought will find its place. Started thinking I was important, if fuzzy.

Both of them speak in terms of these, not to sing their personal victory but to mark the extent of their defeat. the difference between them is revealed in what follows.

These simple words with which Abelard records her feelings vibrate with truth and sincerity. But it can easily happen, even when writing original texts rather than transcriptions, that we commit errors of repetition, because our thoughts and their transmission do not always proceed at the same rate, and the writer can have the mistaken impression that he [sic] still has to write down something that he [sic] has in fact already written.

This is why they can be believed; and no one who believes them can ever judge them as severely as they judge themselves or refuse to grant them what they hoped for in confiding in us, a little love and a little pity. Notions of that sort are fundamentally false. But even on the hypothesis of an intial item of misinformation, we only transfer the problem to an earlier date; at the origin of the error there will always be a 'slip' committed in this case, not by the subject, but by his [sic] written or oral 'informant'.

DENNIS DENISOFF

A Comprehensive Miner Murders the Power Source

the train of miners
the steam of slit thigh in snow
stick match
bushels and bushels of black oily hair
"Look, a union. A union!"
then look at that

the emperor
left hand lightly over right
mistaking the breeze for a camouflage
mistaking my whispers for patchouli
political viburnum
the train of time
snowed in from Albany to Montréal
by dent of cheek
light years from the closest satellite photo
I came to the realization that would determine the course

snowed in
tiny miners
scrape frost off the night
veins pulse as I tap "m"
I tap "m" and the four and twenty elders
fall down pummelled

wait wait wait
Who wants to know and
why do you keep asking?
one starts a commotion and we all do it
that's how fault works
if we *all* do it, nobody gets blamed

my name all over it
my word given (to make order, I say
Henry Mary Lady Jane Grey
enamoured and alluding
vial of veronal
spillikin flaming

A little letter with "Still alive in New York. Scrapers up to here. A cigarette burn in the red carpet of the eleventh floor of the Carlton belongs to me. The ochre girders within the bowels of liberty. Or was it your absence. I'll tell you later. Later, I will be able to tell."

we are so exhaustive
you must not milk the words
we expect a lot in so few
days my slim veined foot
crushes opaque and white
linen juices
reduced to powder
words as flat as sheets of flesh
as transient as breath
and hush and still
a measure of barley for a penny
and three measures of barley for a penny
commerce whispers over me
this then is not salvation
is a late night transformation
from morality to ideology

pumice scrubbed
    ugly American cities roll off like kid dirt: Plattsburg Yonkers
    Saratoga Springs. Not all American cities are ugly. There are
    some further east I heard tell about.
give the vial a trial run
the train pierces the border with me
saying holy holy holy lord god almighty
which was and is and is to come watching
the steel toilet with its capped fluttering
"Elizabeth, James, then parliament"
purse strings taut

metal hands and shoulder blades
flat against the back wall
humming
waiting
humming
(as the emperor's turn to drink from the goblet approaches
lips pursed to a hummingbird
we have exhausted much in so few
all the Oranges for example
James then William and Mary then Anne was it Anne?
James's son

each eats steadily with marked action of jaws
a coiffed head cocked appears as alert as a bottle

> and the number of them was ten thousand times ten thousand
> and thousands of thousands. All water-skiers. All aflock, a chain
> of arms bending at the pit. As the glass is raised and shimmering.
> Him humming. And the numbskulls waiting in and out of the
> shadows chomping at the bit. Letters of cheer dripping prema-
> turely from their lips

left hand lightly over right alabaster fingers kneed
extended languishing
everything so glowing, white and sectioned
between 1879 and the winter
George George George George Victoria

very fortunate life" (as his sister-in-law later called it).)

tense cream calf over the bidet
crisp head lolling on enamel
along a small community of miners
this was happening and we were there

> Gravel for canaries. Marrow for dogs. Grovel for cherries. In as
> much as he could never or hoped for. Black oil on that thigh
> groove. Eels lounging, smoking, anxious for Elizabeth's death.
> And their power was to hurt men five months.

nature obscured by insufficient medical information
the artist at a distance painting by flashlight
the golden miners lolling muscles in Sudbury (Oh,

that is where they do that. Oh, that is *why* I did this) to the rhythm of
Edward George Edward George Edward Elizabeth. Hard drop of
honey dew melon. The emperor's dry lips part and exhale. What was
that he said? *Who* replaces him? The goblet shimmers for moments

and the SKIES open for Michael
the voice of the harpers harping with their harps
every last one of them water-skiers
white linen briefs with wide elastic waistbands
the train: "Klein Calvin Klein Calvin Klein Calvin Klein"
the station itself silent and gentle
frozen flanks
everyone asleep and breathing
while I sprinkle patchouli
in strategic corners

ROBERT MITTENTHAL

Empires of Late

Share the product or read
the flames, if you will
of order. They call these
things letters – autonomous objects that
cannot compete. He said you
have fifteen minutes to organize
the emotions. But if there
is no time for a
human theatre, where is the
theatre where technology electrifies the
people. Or where for a moment
production stops producing machines.
These icons are all contradictions.
Textures that seem to say
spirit functions as a static.
But where the real is
a ratio of history, malfunctions
manage themselves. Against the dominant
too little symptoms an inverse
cripple stands on its ear
to throw light off foreheads
of a number. Is it
a thumb to nose totality
marches to the capital where
on the seventh day no

sun. Or where behind words
a world focused until the
fire bugs and ceases. Beware:
desires rubberstamp is near. I
don't need to give anyone
a blank page. Is this
the knowledge factory where the
blood on my hands bursts
to capacity? Or a lived-in
factory where fear is for
sale. Welcome to my mirror.
After all, work formed with
a typo called "reason." Listening
the words might say, stop
thinking. Thinking the word might
say, is an excuse for
being. But bathed in the
frame, a body wants to
be tolerated. Off your behalf
an object monopolized and ends.
It's the secret of a
point everywhere stopped, empty even
of itself. But please, I'm
wasting your time. I met
you at Forbidden City. You
were ruptured by pretension or
offset for quick sale. I
was SWM – HWP, a new
person transported, shifter with a
harder job. You wore adjectives

advertising lack of time. Black
leather jacket, blonde and proud
of an infantile impulse. I
know this is to start
in the dark but I'm
not euphoric only programmed to
induce the problem in my
hand. This trajectory of names
leads to a kind of sculpted menu in pursuit of
a fiction both nowhere and
unavoidable. Between pockmark and pocket
veto, I went away to see
where fractions must be reduced.
But neither box is silent.
I'll take this passive necklace
to parade before you. All
rise. Lacking short range concrete
gods, the meeting is now
adjourned. Thus, success is defined
against us. But we keep
our weapons clean. In the
theatre of kicked assets, men
and women – in a plastic
bag – carry pictures, tossing pigskins
to pin point spreads of
the wound, to carefully sound
out of the house organ.
We look up upon the
pixels used against us, in
other words, against this one

brief lights out before the
eyes last taste of salt
and pepper. The noise of
a gray scale in short
verse. A coin of this
first time of confused accounts.
The luckiest man is bathed
in electrons. Ionization is the
jolt or the resist of
a second tongue. Finally, missiles
abridge refigured ground. I read
the trees falling down. I
read **the exaggerated birds**. I
read **the long sound in
an invisible ear**. I read
the disclaimer you tied to
a tree, out of a
dictionary too terrible to hang
from self-esteem. The visible body
unworked its wings into a
handful of voices we can't
hear. It's the fallen head
of a collective flash. Gunshots
follow. Gunshots and so forth.

from Martyr Economy

anti-prologue

> If right phrase the
> left out – what fault
> whose truth allows it
> & who is now or
> what ripe eyes me
> (or) what water this
> not small enough

I

Evolutionary? The same harmful
Warming as an avenue orders
Asphalt locks 'til the road bolts

It is the long walk enclosed
A very *he* land – between states
Where description fits what data affords

A lifetime spent approaching the building
Entering slots. If you can draw the horse
It is impossible to ride

Abstracted
The door is a uniform I am
A celebration of interrupts

If the liquid stops here, what diet
What data thrashed
Until vowels cover their holes

What chance storms over action
Until the person pronounced has
Nothing to do with you

2. The folklore of capitalism

In which it is without
without learning to sway the lessens

In which hierarchy affects
the great and small

In which stumbling feet first
selfishness is learned

In which use personified
is its own point of view

In which polar words it is
difficult to know

In which ceremony
an individual thinks (*no way*)

In which trust engaged
to look so organized

In which posterity is a play
on impertinence

3

Escaped wheel and garrote
… studied and took pain

Success is the breed of advanced looks
to finish a kiss of believing

A daily ration, a great light
The landscape – each part
whose lips thirst to grant
by blood so great a name

4

Away from books is the general
storm, a French idea for something
sought. The steam guillotine
seen through the museum window

Just as Plato's house could not be moved
Rome was not built, but polished

Now that glue is on the planet's page,
poets no longer dwell in other words
Animal tracks detach what lies
hidden on earth. Money becomes
memory or vice versa. The mind
becomes a terrible thing
hollow to the call of paper's bag

This wall and frame
is a game of charred bodies, a torture
that rocks the scissored drift

Is it Daphne's escape – a tree
in the present pain – or Apollo
ground into logic, flattened by gaze,
petrified and ready to eat?

5. A way of lying

> *words become the martyrs, the comedians*
> – G. Hartmann

Opinion is not directly
or we have already dealt

Yes, at this time
        mental reservation *for two?*
Interrogated as long as
true – this exercise in appearance
                does not match

I say the word *no* no longer
and have that defective
theory whose bullets show where
no remedy of openness usually is

The confidence is other
most embracing or elusive
veneer of the genuine
It is all the same dogma

Scantily clothed in easy rationale
The unexpressed will subverts
that addition in the mind
with the power to arrest

Each period conversely
outside the house
as if the ears of the question
divide who explains from within

NANCY SHAW

Hair In a Knot

King and fool
hair in a
knot pins wooden
pricks I will
confess flatter my
self stop up
the mouth of.

A warm
overweening
enforce their
least they
were sin
blanket loin.

Harmless divulge
an ace in
a hole the
tripped pretty
plumb we
conceal nothing
under hats.

Hold onto
faction a
knee of a
horse sort
of specious
here for
devotion.

A prima donna's
entrance a
dictionary of
objects fame
knowledge and
fortune good
weather stops.

A tale of
villainy passion
and blood
and things
or harmless
divulge a
woman in
britches here
for devotion.

Sundered direct
suddenly applause
conspired in
favour tied
in a knot
here for
the future.

Forbidden
gloves sacred
blunder salient
tress master
the household
I'd rather
a thousand
times over
than you
you rode
the block.

Donkey skin
a fox's
tactics perched
in a tree
beak of
cheese hard
for the
more or less.

Arrived on the
porch stoop just
a little too
straight forced
him to stammer
embellished too
late.

Have you
ever encountered
flattered self
love glance
amended his
role as
banker host
decoy and
snake.

Suddenly struck
by snow
to wit.

Vain vagabond
coaxing embalm
in tones of
seduction virtue
and fortune
rise and fall
a grande
dame refuses
lavishly obscure.

An honest woman
all guilty
embellish treachery
violence and
vengeance a
habit in
short.

Scour your
body cold
disdain to
regain her
composure on
an advance
encounter a
trifling too
violent connoisseur
of fugitive
biker gothic.

Paste and ointment
bore stigmata
legitimate bride
a culpable
seduction entice
to ruin
brilliant indulgence
glut natural
wane of majesty
solemn profligate
as if every
unfull nature.

Charge suspicion
acts in
seduction
immediate ravish
glean frenzy.

Amorphous
seizure at first
glance obliged
covered his
imaginary blade
learn that
every flatterer
a thousand
times over
in a low
altered voice.

In Doubt a Rose Is a Grotesque Thing

The property line
extends to the
shore line
a dead otter
fish buoys
and driftwood.

I meant nothing by this remark.

In the interest of easing
erotic life. Fur and velvet.

In the attic
a scene of undressing
that describes the patient's life
in the language of flowers.
This was the first assertion
of her still uninhibited animosity.

With an illusion to a gift or contagion.

As you know
this is the first time
I have regretted
meeting famous personalities
miles from home.

But instead I have chosen
to investigate cadavers
perhaps a hunting scene.

Because I was reared in a hothouse
a final euphemism:
The illusion did not last.

For more than a week
failing the obvious
I was fed up with memories.

This is much more than scenery.

In a waiting room
where a picture on a wall
could spell revenge.

If I may suppose
the scene of the kiss
took place in this way.
But it was not until
the incident by the lake
that we were encouraged
and forced to make confessions.

The younger of the two was the stranger.

In a seemingly endless, paranoid view
of events, I watched from a room I
knew too well on a slender
riotous island.

With his life and mind under daily dissection.

My libidinal compliment
just as one
might refer to
inner landscape.

She'd come east in a fashion
that rather took your breath away.
Aspiring to be
the originator of moments.

There is no need for discretion.
A tremendous attraction.
An elegant adversity.

I am a natural runner.

As if a rock hit you
several times
on the head.

Familiar as it may be.

A national betrayal.
A snap of cold weather.
A hard-luck story.
Hailed with a passion.

The Illusion Did Not Last

It began harmlessly with a question:
Who was counter-nature?

After this highly discursive introduction
another small anecdote:
at intervals of an hour
each believed herself
the true heroine.

Supposing she fell into a frenzy
somewhere between
the wish and its fulfillment.

Rumours, and rumours of rumours.
Volumes of heresy.

No longer young
as he once was
the arsonist.

Episodic testimony.

The man on whom the heavy burden
had fallen had no feeling for sights
signalling peril everywhere
in a hectic show of civility.
I thought this was typical

Later, several burning barrels of cordiality.

At least they do not notice
it in themselves
the reading of
a good life
the heroic man
bravely lashing.

Dim sheath;
that I suddenly felt this.

PETER CULLEY

Winterreise
after F. Schubert and W. Müller

Out of salt, iron
    and out of iron, gold
and out of gold
    along the chain
of alchemical time reversals
    the endless valley of rock
cools and twists
    into its dear
and familiar contours;
    arbutus buttress
the hillside, black-faced
    hogs take their ease
beneath the pale sun, a rumbling
    truck ejects a gnarled and burly
knob of firewood
    into the roadway,
and each day
    he consults the compass
to find magnetic north
    has drifted a few degrees
off true –
    and so
with the deep inner radar
    all humans possess, inscribed

on their dna roughly
    as are these words on this
piece of paper –
    he sets off
into deepest winter.
    As the northern beacon
transformed into sugar
    halts in its journey
across the deep lake of matter, through
    the lumbar towards articulation
and action, he hesitates
    beneath the byzantine struts
of the railway station, uncertain
    of which sparrow
to feed and from which sparrow
    to ask directions –
northwards, leaf-eating insects
    green, bark-feeders
mottled grey; grouse
    the colour of heather;
dwarfed shells
    in the brackish waters
beyond, stunted and monstrous
    past the tree-line.
Low streak
    of platinum
edg'd with pewter, pumpkin holler
    forward straggle
of quasi-suburban
    foreground, graffiti

outside Turku announces
   welcome to fucktown.

Anecdotal evidence
   a mock tectonic plate
on which
   the hapless aspirant
stands as one
   upon a surfboard crossing
the lake of fire,
   a geologist
tut-tutting over
   a particularly disappointing
core sample –
   yet still he hovers
in half-sleep
   thickened sun of late afternoon
a throbbing and
   a flickering
through the low forest;
   neat huts, a leaning water tower –
frosted fern and nettle spread
   along the cutbank
presage the descent
   from warm kitten enclosure
to the ironic
   and angular avenues
of the city
   of diminished expectation.

Destroyed and sectioned
    tamarack into a crude
pyramid in the yard, floating
    ridge of fir indexed somewhere,
ready for the hot tip
    of the landlord's cigarette,
unreconstructed altar
    of cool brick and
rusted rack, a fat
    coot cracks
a dead branch.
    Beyond the fence
it is drab impulse
    and bitter consumption –
soundtrack, head cleaner,
    kerosene, protein;
from the narrow window
    Friedrich's Christ
just barely visible
    on his mountaintop, still
writhing in the warm searchlight
    of late summer.

A Letter From Hammertown to
East Vancouver and the East Village

dear K. –

I'm planning ahead
    for the first time –

for soon it will be spring
    and then it will be the grid of appearance

upon which spring can be laid.
    That is, what is from the ground up
    becoming

will be from the ether
    managed –
        the lawns will fade to unfenced ochre,

back onto alleys, roughly narrow paved
    (the width of an Austin

from the administration of Macmillan)
    the poignant sheds will sprawl and lean

another season
    for no reason.

But all of this, though hardly molecular,
    – if squinted at through eyes oracular –

betrays conclusions scarcely singular:
　　the scale is still a cap full of cabbage

resting on a bag of flesh
　　pulled along by a little red wagon –

what eventually emerges
　　from dirty stubby fingers toes
　　　　beggars description

but is no secret either.

　　A deer trail,
　　　　then a dog trail,
　　　　　　then Pete's trail,

then my trail. Sherpa Tensing sits puffing
　　on the roof of the world –

his belief in process absorbed
　　by the throbbing worm

that mutters and sweats
　　at the mucky heart
　　　　of being …

Thus engaged,
　　rhetoric becomes prosthesis,

staggers down the parade route
　　of a strange city
　　　　within a giant face of plaster –

but speak!
       it does not.

Another grotesquerie
   affirming
      the shapeliness of all things – likewise

the saturate flowers, the seepage
   suspect, the coffee grounds
      idling in the tray – such that

progressive collapse seems itself a tender unfolding,
   a rose within a bible drying,
      a whiff of distant evening cooking…

The winter twilight's pall of woodsmoke
   drifts and softens

even as it sears and conceals –
   just as the low millennial fog of Hammertown
      cloaks the shuttered factories, dog-ridden lots and

oil-dappled pavements
   in the wispy raiments
      of authenticity…

I stirred the pondwater
   with a little stick, watched
      duckweed swirl

as though beneath
    February's late ice, while
        through the bright fractal enclosures

of the alder grove
    flickers flicked, towhees wheeled
        tanagers managed –

I'm lining things up
    all in a little row
        so that the real image of spring

and the mental image of spring
    can be made to somehow agree –

the new incorporated self
    erects a kind of recording scrim, on which
        the successive domed apprehensions
            of the April sky, the

broiling surface tension of Dodd Narrows, etc.
    can be decelerated and examined –

a field guide to fields, a boy's book of burls,
the unexamined yard, fern monochrome attribution,
dull days in the eastern capitals…

    the index: the big one

these wet streets, your hands

plunged into the warm dirt, the exhaust fans
    of the endless orange tunnel that lies between us,

what of them?
    I try to think of you
       and can bring to mind
         only the great parabolic bridges
       in whose shadow you live, fist-sized rivets
        of red iron, buoying above
       the molten stream of thought

into which
    each day you are thrown!

As the day grows clear and cold
    the mind grows hazy, the wind indicating
       woodpecker hesitates
    and reverses; the earth, like a little
       boat on a calm day
    pitches and rolls, a metal stylus

on a resonating film
    of charged oil …

Fruit Dots

in May. As it unfolds
    spores are discharged.
Tuft of rusty wool

above the fruiting pinnae,
    shallow vase formed, flooded
the woods with golden light.

Other osmundas, absence of the
    fertile fonds. Erect,
curving outward,

oblong-lanceolate; obtuse divisions
    taller than sterile
entire or toothed.

Of the midrib, indusium delicate –
    little fronds, ecstatic presence
of the deeper woods.

Arched across the rock-broken
    stream, carpeted with low;
where precious red-cupped mosses

stretch basswood overhead
    cliff which forms.
Early meadow rue –

lobed and rounded leaflet
    crowds to the roadside
moist hollows: fronds

tremulous on their black
    chance to be driving
by a bank overgrown,

possessed by a tormenting love
    sadly state but firm;
aloofness which adds

haunts are dim.
    Summit of the slender
black and polished, recurved

branches bearing
    several slender,
under margin of a lobe

dotted with fragrant heaps.
    Entered the cool
shade, beauty and luxuriance,

rich green arched above
    rigid fruit clusters.
Crown firmed rigid;

by means of underground runners
    crawled under
a tight board fence –

free veins with simple veinlets
        do not reach
the midvein. Reflexed marginal

rows of bright brown sporangia
        wedged in neighbouring
crannies, sprang from limestone cliffs;

so blended, with their rocky
        self-assurance at variance.
Prostrate among the rocks

rise the firm
        graceful crowns:
conspicuously marginal

fruit-dots, caudex covered by the bases –
        apex and the tips
of its pinnules, plumes

of departing summer,
        of the greenhouse.
Above the black leaf-mould

immortal in the swamp herbage,
        centre shades away
less chaffy stalks; mossy ledges

above star-like stumps of decaying.
        A projecting shelf
of bluish green;

leathery, tapering,
    decayed at its tip
a flower yet unnamed.

Day count.
    Columbine flings out
just uncurled

roots of some great
    nodding blossom,
among which the stream forces,

flavoured with the essence
    once more.
Fastened underneath

into jagged, spreading –
    were it not for the difference
twice to thrice-pinnate

finally appear naked,
    early withering and exposing
beneath a reflexed portion.

Green takes on
    a dark heraldic eagle
in a cross-section of the young stalk:

does not wither away,
    grown by reason of the licking.
Shall shellfish

in the Andes at fourteen feet
    widely spreading at the summit?
Reflexed edge, somewhat open

borne in a continuous line;
    stout stalk, from the trunks
somewhat lustrous –

upward turning
    on their upper
through the winter.

In the rocky woods
    having shiny scales
convex; persistent

along the roadside
    and in wet,
found in the tiniest

its creeping rootstock rise.
    At times wear very light,
standing brown and dry

from early frosts –
    form midway
in masses – in wet meadows

inappropriateness, wavy-toothed
    divisions; berry-like bodies
usually heart-shaped.

Scattered on the lower surface
    shale, and conglomerate
near limestone cliffs

sprays of the bulblet
    turreted summits.
Rigid grace, slim in crowded ranks,

into moist ravines
    necessitates the twisting
of its stalk. Shelves of shaded rocks:

surprise – combination of delicacy,
    black stemmed
under groups of red, with blackish

and shining, silvery till maturity,
    base auricled;
the tangle of wild

close to the roadside fence.
    Of some amber-coloured brook
the wild bergamot

its swift noiseless flow.
    Uncurl in May –
present a rather blotched

delicacy, scarlet cluster,
    background. Of grain shine
between umbrella-like Brakes:

so recently unfolded texture
    seems a trifle.
Close against the rails;

as the curves and dimples,
    little undulations
of the August woods' border –

Of course I didn't know about it before I heard about it so
in that way I did start it

KSW

Kisses So Wet

When I started the Kootenay School or Writing everybody
told me we'd be bankrupt within a week. Never enough toilet
paper, or a way to keep the door shut.
solos/duets/choruses/panel discussions

And Dan Farrell loaded me his l=a=n=g=u=a=g=e
You still have it. I   where that was.

Someone else who did not start it
Or attend many meetings
but who took a fence
and wondered if weather
was right
or underhanded
had housedresses
and wore them convincingly
like a house sapphire
had a wringer washer
risking fingers
to pressure out
and popped

her dirty colloquialisms
for all to bear
feeding the laundry through rollers (ringers), turning it back
into clothing. The excess water fell to a pan on the floor and
guests were surprised to remember their mothers
not that long ago
what funny pleasure to get from harder bother
the outdated machine of involvement
processing the materials
dry dirty – wet clean – damp flat

And Dee would say its not up to any body, certainly not Kisses
So Wet, being only the sum of its individual's fictions to grant
me credit
But that's not what I thought I meant by surprised that they
noticed me but unto another rather neither might not other-
wise would I have found such an idea

Somehow silver services stand in for relations and arrows for
language and lips for communication and handshakes for love
and melted butter for acceptance and over-stuffed pillows for
understanding and big asses for empathy and footprints for
interest and eyebrows for involvement and timeframes for
closeness and inseams for intimacy and zippers for unity and
eggs for togetherness and branches for all the aching

Our band was called Kisses So Wet and everyone including us
thought that was a stupid name. But it had an appalling neu-
trality that suited our disagreeability. We didn't create music
but misery. As neither were necessary and misery was cheaper

we chose that. Our first practices were carried out above the old General Testing Laboratories office. She was our leader and couldn't care less but we knew with so much misery in the world there would be a lot of competition. And though her father owned the station we had to bribe petty officials to get venues to hold our misery loves company nights. Misery was increased by random killings, surprise chemical spills, false emotions and copy-cat crime. But people complained, whined, droned, "I could do that" the implication being that their ability disqualified our activity as art. Still, we weren't really, authentically, miserable. Our magazine "in praise of wounds that never heal" became a hit with pre-teens. We tried to get indignant, feel misunderstood, used, abandoned, but actually we understood.

We didn't play any instruments so we couldn't get good at them. We showed slides and films and amplified the sounds of different bodily functions.

Now our ideas from that time return like carriages drawn & coiffeured a way and a reason and often seeing a wrong done in the implausible shadow of the really big guns. Ironsides so steep miners went down on donkeys, but who would come to their resort. Still singing through the indented hedges or justified boulders or left aligned footlongs were all the tones and turns of passage encountered, meaning much new territory in the air. Just button and drink and vomit and redden and thin and purse and mistake and decide and steady and it was simpler then and leave unintentionally.
vacuuming

A way through signifiers sanctifiers and scatologues
and even after dinner
Which I could never muster not dinner but anything after
she reads

And, like a community if only we wanted to be together and
like a family I've got to go; I'm in past curfew again

When the old heroes and mentors started dying off the not so
younger generation got nervous and started taking positions.
They worried, what will we bring? The last thought, luck. Said,
he brought modernism. Brought modernism to Vancouver.
What forward can we bring to the backward? What zest for
life? But then is acceptance a virtue or just a refusal to take a
stand.

No one warned her that he was insane because those who
knew thought it was evident and those that didn't, couldn't

Everything she says doesn't go without saying away

Something in her gets annoyed at his sound poem. Like a burr
under the saddle his fits don't sit right. Like a car alarm no one
cares about he goes off again
to warm off breached perimeters.

When I started the Kootenay School of Writing
I thought I was right
When I started the Kootenay School of Writing
I thought I was alone
When I started the Kootenay School of Writing
I thought we were together
that day
that meeting
the moment when

the time passed the desire lurched forward absolutely South
Eastern Inquiry Through Waving at the Moment Memory
Opens the Nonurban Academy as Speech

it was in the evening going up the stairs someone had told me
about it and I set off the Broadway Room from That One or
Thing Which Is Inscribing

it was in the evening going up the stairs someone had told me
about and I set off the Stan Douglas Artist's Talk and Laiwan's
Flowers Institute of Surround

it was in the evening going up the stairs someone had told me
about and I walked into The Room Which Was Too Full had
any classes been offered by this time later comes We Compos-
ing Thinking

it was in the evening going up the stairs someone had told me
about and I saw through the doorway Stan bent over a slide
projector Every One Was Facing Forward Senior Secondary
Which Has as its Purpose Inscription

it was in the evening going up the stairs someone had told me about and It Was Hard To Concentrate Because of the Crowd/Place Where Some are In Charge of Giving to Others a part of What's Now Often Done With Computers

It was later me again up three flights of stairs with urine at the bottom that I'd been up before when the now Ping Pong Club had served as a location for gigs and seen D.O.A. and wondered about emergency exits door at the north end of the corridor Been There many Times Not the Building But the Idea landmark from which Often Starts In Adolescence as a Diary

for Deanna Ferguson, July 1994

JEFF DERKSEN

Interface

I needlessly mapped an occasion, splitting my support, serving myself.

A north, a south pointing pronouns in pockets.

"Ordinary people were saying 'We want to be free'."

Higher Alert.

The return for refund where applicable part was never clear, but we continued, stopping at each gas station to ask.

Liberal pride harnesses a portion, and I'd prefer not to comment on my name.

"Sweet Dave" written in black felt pen on the back of his yellow rain slicker.

The fish instinctively know where the international boundaries are.

The dupe quotient seemed to apply so clearly to me that I had to leave the table.

Soviet Union 24.9%.

A pinched nerve or an upper rib took away all enjoyment of the available technology.

I was humped like a salmon.

Terminal Carpal Tunnel syndrome.

"We can see a day when borders will mean nothing more than knowing where to cut your lawn."

I had been puking at the announcement but then stopped, seeing no profit in it.

Evil in a nasally way, with a hundred miles of barbed wire, but once in the workplace an agenda smoothed over the whole thing.

The structure I hate also hates me, but it makes me, and that's where the problem starts.

I peeled back the wrapping on the bag of ethnic paper clips.

The demographics preceded me.

United States 18.3%.

"Sell abroad or go under" is forced from the drop in domestic arms needs.

We sought to mollify the sulking with a buy-out plan – I could hardly hold on when it got slippery.

The black chairman of the Joint Chiefs of Staff.

A kind of horned-up atmosphere saturated the bank line-up, snaking through the blue velvet corral.

Interface of self and place passes me through a translation machine.

But when my left eye is jumping, I don't know where I'm at.

The car horn punctuates the trumpet solo.

How could I talk about a brush stroke?

Even though the ultra-sonic image of my testicle was on the split screen right in front of me, I felt detached, cube- or kiosklike.

Through hard work and volunteer effort a pragmatics began to arise: how does it translate to I really really care about whatever.

A strike that tries to "inconvenience the public as little as possible."

The guys in the car gave a polite honk, as if embarrassed by such a coded response.

Every team has to have a grinder, I just thought it would never be me.

"Males have strange and elaborate paired crab-clawlike jointed appendages attached to the snout, which had a sexual function; the females are unencumbered."

It was a bonspiel I could hardly support, even as a decent tax dodge.

Great Britain 17.1%.

"It's only with plain talking, and a give and take on both sides, that will ensure there are forests in the future."

The high-pitched hum started to hurt, but we decided not to say anything.

Propaganda points to propaganda within a transparent frame.

The translation process that ends with "Harvesting the necks of the infidel aggressors."

Pure desire arrives like a train – on rails.

Seallike, barking and clapping, tilting and rolling my head back until they agreed to take the unpaid portion off the bill.

"Urgent Fury" wasn't the movie, but the code name: Grenada 1983.

It was a cynical attempt at inclusion, based almost entirely on family background – just said no to a regionalism of noses.

But once the embarrassment blew we actually talked, balking at a paradise subsidy.

Then the letter returned replied with a quirky formality, like viewing another culture from a deaf ethnographic point of view.

Something like postcolonial packaging taken personally in a

resource-based economy; I look out my window and see history *versus* I look out my window and see a window.

Visually complicated, overlapping and lapsing.

Small, polished engine parts that still look usable, but which are unidentified for any function.

Bush's "approval rating" is 87%, the highest for any president since Roosevelt: February 1991.

I wanted to argue but was locked into my role of simply trying to be nice, or to conciliate an agreement, so I just tapped on the glass and walked away.

There was a picture of him "in the field," notebook in hand, informant at knee.

"A picnic not a potlatch."

A layered invention, looking in its own window.

That binding arbitration of lip to neck or hips to hoola hoop.

France 8.9%.

It was bad news coming even from a hundred miles away *or*, after adapting, we grew to like the rattlesnake necktie.

The percentage of blacks in the U.S. Armed Forces is higher than many other industries – this was talked about as a progressive step.

Apparently they'd been doing it like that for years.

A used car-battery sells for $1.50.

One hundred and thirty-eight pounds of joy.

It was a way of thinking about myself that took in all perspectives and appeared not to damage the environment.

Those small, see-through fish seemed a good model.

I won't say that the imperialism placated me, but that the stroking of the consumer goods really calmed me down.

And an eel-skin briefcase as a signing bonus.

"Power is frequently understood as force personified" and the pronouns disclose this.

An intensity in menus, the pivotal moment.

The U.S.S. Meyerkord docked in Vancouver before going on to the Gulf.

Oil-proof and $69.95.

I kept my head down and pedalled the machine faster, the air of sexuality getting thick.

Bright and long-lasting negative effects of Cartesian perspectivalism on viewing our own bodies from the head down.

Two elections, about a hundred days of rain and it will be spring.

It's a made position, like a pewter spoon or a leather letter opener.

The Rocket Richard riots would be an example of spontaneous agency.

"Jeanine is a living example of Noranda's attitude to employees."

China 6.3%.

This train.

The residual anger resides here [points with right hand] and accumulates here [points with left hand], I'm still looking for the spigot.

More American soldiers were killed by accidents during the build-up than by either the Iraqi army or so-called friendly fire.

Generic or genetic.

Sapped like a sap machine.

There are so many *ones* I want to be – beyond the cardboard maquette stage, more at the prototype level, the "working model" example.

A subject-in-process with a horn section.

Rent context.

By the book legally and with the compassion of the United Fruit Company.

Every device will have its homecoming.

"We may not have all the right answers, but we have the right car."

At no point in Canadian history has a federal government been so unpopular: January 1991.

Counter-top culture.

The silent trajectory of the fist gave me time to think, opened the local to a national identity with blinkers on.

Anxiety punctuated by time.

West Germany 5.4%.

"I'm a man – spell it *I apostrophe M*."

Patience dispersed through the legs lead me to "I become my job" now I'm pulling together like white blood cells.

The language of war at this juncture is an aim, a name.

If history is the memory of time what would our monument be?

The semiotics of hair shows me a socially saturated sign and I engage at the primary level of meaning.

General failure of hippies.

By extension I am engaged in war, driving my car or taking one on the chin.

Nonunion job structure creamed my attention span.

The U.S. Navy did phone to apologize, making me feel even more like a nation, more unlike the United Nations, but still a little sore in the jaw.

They wanted to argue generations, but the past year is all archives.

"In the Canadian Grain Elevator."

There is an incredible amount of natural beauty and we engage with it accordingly!

Step down from the cockpit and give your name, hometown, and stock response as a universal narrative.

So-called air-superiority writers.

A highly developed national sense of irony was in place by 1942: Canadian raid on Dieppe was code named Operation Jubilee.

Now I become my own lunch special.

Pin-point accuracy, with the "pin" being a building.

Italy 5.4%.

I see traces of my labour mechanically reproduced and it makes me *happy*.

A generic ethnocentrism made it "everybody's town" with a blank default.

The highly competitive profession of proofreading.

I took the initiative personally so sought the etymology of *basket-case*.

A lifetime achievement award that doubles as an ashtray when laid flat.

I still answer the phone as if I were "employed": that reminds me that the structure you hate, hates you.

General Schwarzkopf's verse, although having a clarity of tone, lacks formal innovation.

Blowing off steam implies a natural build-up and then release rather than rage.

Like a pig through a python.

I wonder, would a matchbox hold my subjectivity?

Lieutenant-Colonel Butt phoned me at work to assure me of his regrets on the "unfortunate incident" and the strictness of the naval code.

Books float.

Japan 3.5%.

One abdication, two resignations, an erasing of the electoral memory and it will be spring.

I enter the artist's body of work by walking across Second and Cambie, becoming a flâneur in modernism at the shutter's click.

The body could be pure pleasure – floating in an isolation tank.

The brine shrimp of the family.

"Operation Comfort" lacks irony in not recognizing an alternative system: comparative literature without the *comparative*.

The stacking of so-called psychological damage has me at the crossroads rather than the keyboard – manifest in tissues or fish scales laminated to a role model.

Or it's the neocolonial model that makes us humble, optimistic, plaid.

At this point, rather than tying, I'm trying to [quote] enjoy my life [end quote] whether it's eight and a half by eleven or quarter after twelve.

The bay curves past the family beach and pier, crosses the 49th Parallel, and terminates in an oil-tanker dock and naval base.

Sweden 2.5%.

Sexual activity displaces my stomach upward by an inch.

The fleshy space where the hyphen was between *work* and *place*.

Six months before a presidential election, Bush is tied with a candidate who is, as yet, officially undeclared: June 1992.

Baltics as a dictionary entry is the victory of context over text.

I bought your book for a quarter.

My body's attached to my leg, to a genetic history, to a parallel sentence structure stretching over the horizon.

"A reader must face the fact that Canadian Literature is undeniably sombre and negative, and that this to a large extent is both a reflection and a chosen definition of the national sensibility,"

Cheerleading is a growth industry in the U.S.

I'm stepping aside here, just to say that if it's not my job, I'm not going to do it, and if it's not my arm I won't twist it.

A relegation of last week to a distant and unconnected past, an increase in the amount of "paid political announcements" on TV, the end of the salmon season, and it will be fall.

My world, myopia.

"*The* car is *a* extension of you."

A dread feeling, linked with time, becomes the experience of [quote] the quotidian [end quote], so I'm a fragment reading up to see when I was whole.

A serf in his serfdom.

Operation Desert Shield, Operation Just Cause, Operation Rolling Thunder, Operation Success, Operation Martyrdom, Operation Should We Be Doing This?

Crosstown traffic is classist as well as racist.

I would like to "jump out of my skin."

Official national animal.

"I honestly want to restore Kuwait's international borders."

The space between *dismal* and received knowledge is where "popular culture" steps in.

Post-election morning coincides with the first frost and the plants have a shocked, trampled look.

Poland 2.3%.

The one and the frenzy.

A pair of shoes on top of a rock in an empty lot where there once was a house.

I'm returning after an extensive guitar solo.

Cranes dot the skyline in an homage to the domination of *economic* over *place* – it is unbuilt business I'm talking about, the Pacific Rim lapping at my ankles.

Unemployment went up in the U.S. during the war.

It's too easy to attach a possessive apostrophe to mass-produced products, so I'll end here.

"Racism has no place in the battlefield."

Dominant tropes won't allow me to buy tripe."

I carry context with me and become tourism.

A Bibliography

GERALD CREEDE *Ambit*, Tsunami Editions, 1993.

PETER CULLEY *The Climax Forest*, Leech Press, 1995.

KEVIN DAVIES *Pause Button*, Tsunami Editions, 1992.

DENNIS DENISOFF *Dog Years*, Arsenal Pulp Press, 1991; *Tender Agencies*, Arsenal Pulp Press, 1994.

JEFF DERKSEN *Down Time*, Talonbooks, 1990; *Dwell*, Talonbooks, 1993. Website: www.lot.at/mynewidea_com.

DAN FARRELL *Ape* (chapbook), Tsunami Editions, 1988; *Thinking of You*, Tsunami Editions, 1994; *Last Instance*, Krupskaya, 1999. Website: www.erols.com/dfar.

DEANNA FERGUSON *The Relative Minor*, Tsunami Editions, 1993; *Small Holdings* (chapbook), Tsunami Editions, 1999; *Rough Bush* (chapbook), Meow Books, 1996; *ddilemma* (chapbook), hole books, 1997; *Available Light*, Coach House Books (forthcoming).

DOROTHY TRUJILLO LUSK *Redactive*, Talonbooks, 1992.

KATHRYN MACLEOD *How Two* (chapbook), Tsunami Editions, n.d.; *Mouthpiece*, Tsunami Editions, 1995.

ROBERT MITTENTHAL *Ready Terms* (chapbook), Tsunami Editions, 1989; *Martyr Economy* (chapbook), Sprang Texts, 1993

JUDY RADUL *Rotating Bodies*, Petarade Press, 1988; *Boner 9190 and the Weak*, Knust Press, 1989; *Character Weakness*, Knust Press, 1993.

LISA ROBERTSON *The Apothecary* (chapbook), Tsunami Editions,
  n.d.; (with Catriona Strang and Christine Stewart) *The Barscheit
  Horse* (chapbook), The Berkeley Horse #49, 1993; *XEclogue, Tsunami
  Editions, 1993, revised edition, New Star Books, 1999; Debbie: An Epic,*
  New Star Books, 1997.

NANCY SHAW *Affordable Tedium* (chapbook), Tsunami Editions, n.d.;
  Scoptocratic, ECW Press, 1993 (with Catriona Strang and Monika
  Kin Gagnon) *The Institute Songbook* (chapbook), The Institute, 1995.

COLIN SMITH *Multiple Poses,* Tsunami Editions, 1997.

CATRIONA STRANG *Tem* (chapbook), Barscheit, 1992; *Low Fancy,*
  ECW Press, 1993; (with Lisa Robertson and Christine Stewart) *The
  Barscheit Horse* (chapbook), The Berkeley Horse #49, 1993; (with
  Nancy Shaw and Monika Kin Gagnon) *The Institute Songbook*
  (chapbook), The Institute, 1995; *Steep: A Performance Notebook,*
  Seeing Eye Books, 1997; (with François Houle) *The Clamourous
  Alphabet* (CD), 1999.

LARY TIMEWELL (BREMNER) *Jump/Cut* (chapbook), Tsunami
  Editions, n.d.

Some addresses

ARSENAL PULP PRESS 103·1014 Homer St., Vancouver, BC
  V6B 2W9; www.arsenalpulp.com.

COACH HOUSE BOOKS www.chbooks.com.

HOLE BOOKS 2664 William St., Vancouver, BC V5K 2Y5.

KOOTENAY SCHOOL OF WRITING 103·400 Smithe St., Vancouver,
  BC V6B 5E4; www.ksw.net.

KRUPSKAYA PO Box 420249, San Francisco, CA 94142-0249.

LEECH BOOKS 1760 W. 2nd Av., Vancouver, BC V6J 1H6.

NEW STAR BOOKS 107·3477 Commercial St., Vancouver, BC V5N 4E8; www.NewStarBooks.com.

OPEN LETTER 499 Dufferin Av., London, ON N6B 2A1. Tenth Series, Number 1, Winter 1998, Disgust and Overdetermination: A Poetics Issue, was guest-edited by Jeff Derksen and contains work by many of the writers in this anthology.

RADDLE MOON / SPRANG TEXTS #518·350 E. 2nd Av., Vancouver, BC V5T 4R8; www.sfu.ca/~clarkd.

RADIOFREERAINFOREST Program on Vancouver Co-operative Radio, CFRO 102.7 fm, hosted by Gerry Gilbert; Sundays at 9 pm. Frequently broadcasts KSW-hosted readings.

SMALL PRESS DISTRIBUTION 1814 San Pablo Av., Berkeley, CA 94702. Source for books by many of the writers included or referred to in this book.

SUBTEXT www.speakeasy.org/subtext. A Seattle reading series that has featured many KSW writers.

TALONBOOKS 104·3100 Production Way, Burnaby, BC V5A 4R4; www.swifty.com/talon/.

TSUNAMI EDITIONS 14-1507 E. 2nd Avenue, Vancouver, BC V5N 1C8. Edited at various times by Lary Bremner, Deanna Ferguson, and Michael Barnholden, Tsunami has published many of the writers in this book.

WESTCOASTLINE 2027 East Academic Annex, Simon Fraser University, Burnaby, BC V5A 1S6. Issue 24/1, Spring 1991, featured many KSW writers.

WRITING   c/o Kootenay School of Writing, 103 · 400 Smithe St., Vancouver, BC   V6B 5E4. Suspended publication in 1992 after 28 issues. Copies of many back issues are still available.